P9-DXL-429

Visiting Edna
and Good for Otto

Also by David Rabe

Visiting Edna
and Good for Otto
Two Plays

David Rabe

Grove Press
New York

First Grove Atlantic paperback edition: August 2017

Published simultaneously in Canada
Printed in the United States of America

FIRST EDITION

ISBN 978-0-8021-2690-0
eISBN 978-0-8021-8960-8

Library of Congress Cataloging-in-Publication data is available for this title.

Grove Press
an imprint of Grove Atlantic
154 West 14th Street
New York, NY 10011

Distributed by Publishers Group West

groveatlantic.com

17 18 19 20   10 9 8 7 6 5 4 3 2 1

Visiting Edna

For Ruth and Jill.

PRODUCTION CREDITS

Visiting Edna was originally produced by the Steppenwolf Theatre Company (Anna D. Shapiro, Artistic Director; Jonathan Berry, Artistic Producer), opening on September 15, 2016, in Chicago. It was directed by Anna D. Shapiro; Scenic Design: David Zinn; Costume Design: Linda Roethke; Lighting Design: Marcus Doshi; Sound Design: Rob Milburn; Original Music: Michael Bodeen; Casting: Tam Dickson; Stage Manager: Christine D. Freeburg.

The cast was as follows, in order of appearance:

ACTOR ONE	Sally Murphy
ACTOR TWO	Tim Hopper
EDNA	Debra Monk
ANDREW	Ian Barford
ACTOR THREE	Michael Rabe

CHARACTERS

ACTOR ONE

ACTOR TWO

EDNA

ANDREW

ACTOR THREE

SETTING   Edna's apartment. 1990s

ACT ONE

The time is the 1990s, EDNA'S apartment in a medium-sized Iowa town. Stage right is a small kitchen area that contains a sink, stove, refrigerator, kitchen table with chairs and a vase of flowers on it, and a little desk beside the refrigerator. The space extends stage left into a living room where a recliner sits beside a small table and faces a TV stand, wooden, but with no actual TV on it, though there is a VCR under it. Nearby shelving holds some VHS tapes. The door to the outside is up center with an alcove between two small rooms, stage left being the door to Edna's bedroom. The interior of Edna's bedroom is a playing space upstage left. This room should meet the needs of playability rather than strict literal architecture. To the stage right of the alcove there is a bathroom door and further along, a door to a second small bedroom, both facing out. These doors are more or less parallel to and behind the kitchen counter and stove. Lamps here and there. Family pictures on the wall. Tokens and cards. A crucifix on the wall. A second recliner has been shoved off to the side. Lights rise on ACTOR ONE, a bright, energetic young woman dressed in a black sweater and slacks, a perky, fun outfit. She enters from stage left and and walks down front, addressing the audience.

ACTOR ONE   I am, as you see, a person. A human being. And given the nature of our relationship—yours and mine—at the present moment—I mean, our spatial relationship—you can safely conclude—in fact you must conclude—that I am an actor. Which I am. At least at the moment. And as an actor, I am to portray—in the play—for the length of the play, I am to portray . . . Television. That's right. Television. I am to act it. I am to act, as an actor, Television. In other words, that's my character. I will be—when you look at me, you will see—"Television." That's what he's written, and so I

7

am ready—I will to the best of my abilities—I mean, "Actor One will portray, television," he writes. And I'm like, you know, well, all right. Sure. Whatever you say. I mean, a part is a part. I'll take it. But then I thought, "now what? Exactly how do I do it?" At first I asked myself, Well, should I pretend to be a box? I mean, should I kind of somehow . . . however . . . box myself? I mean, I thought about wearing a box. Being a box. We all thought about it. We consulted the director, costume designer—we have brainstormed, believe you me . . . and . . . Or, you know, is it rabbit ears? Could it be this sort of hat thing with rabbit ears? Don't be surprised if you see that. Me with rabbit ears. Or . . . maybe a cord, you know, a cable cord or . . . A satellite dish! That's it. I carry it or attach it somehow . . . I don't think he gave the whole thing any real thought. He just had this idea. And so I'll be doing my best. But I'm feeling that it'll all be a sort of—as the saying goes, "a work in progress."

Actor One can sit on the TV stand at times, using elements such as cables, antennae, a satellite dish. Lights, along with coordination with ANDREW or Edna using the remote, can signal when the TV is on or off and create a presence at this location which Actor One can occupy, though at times she can move about as her relationships develop with the characters. There should also be a use of music and sound to enhance her TV presence.

Now as Actor One says, "a work in progress," ACTOR TWO enters from state right. A man, trim, with an intelligent gaze, not without cunning, he wears a black sweater and casual black trousers. He walks down front, addressing the audience.

ACTOR TWO   And I—I am to portray Cancer. That's right. You heard me right. I, too, am a work in progress. Steadily. Secretly. Do you even see me?

A tea kettle whistles and the bathroom door opens and an old woman comes out; she shuffles toward the recliner.

Ah. Here she comes. Edna. My host. Age 78. Back from the bathroom. Congestive Heart failure. Diabetes. Arthritis that feels like a vicious slash beneath her clavicle and down, like a knife through

8

the throat of a sheep. Knees of course, too. Knuckles. Ankles. She's had a colostomy. Diverticulitis that couldn't be reversed. She's just had to irrigate herself. That's where she's coming from. It's a process that has to do with flushing her bowels to avoid these violent cramps. It's an enema of sorts that she has to do twice a week. Only she doesn't have any bowels any more. Not in the conventional sense. And now me—she has me, too—her diagnosis, as she likes to call me. And do you know what? Colostomy. Arthritis. Congestive heart failure, and she's desperate to live. Hungry to live. Praying to live.

As Edna sinks into the chair, Actor Two studies her.

The irrigation . . . leaves her, as you see, exhausted, her heart struggling, all systems debilitated, an opportunity, I would think for me to take a little more advantage. To inch forward. Dig deeper. Pursue my goals. (*looking out*) I mean nothing by it. But already you don't like me. I can tell. It's just what I do. Being what I am.

Edna sits panting. Actor One has been watching, and she leans in toward Edna now.

ACTOR ONE   Edna. I'm here. Right here. Turn me on, why don't you. Wanna watch the news? Or a sitcom? You should watch a sitcom.

The Phone rings, and Edna reaches, picks it up.

EDNA   Hello. Oh. Hello, Bernice. What? No, no. I'm fine. Just worried. You know. I fly with them. If those kids of mine, either one of them are in the air, I'm flying too. What? Really? No. I don't have the damn thing on. (*as she picks up the remote, aims it and turns on the television*) No, no. I didn't hear about that.

ACTOR ONE   (*hurriedly putting on a contraption of rabbit ears on her head*)   Tornadoes ripped through Ashgwago county with devastating two hundred miles-per-hour winds in a savage wedge of violence that left twelve dead and two thousand homeless.

EDNA   That's not our way is it. I mean, it's not headed our way.

ACTOR ONE   Eye witnesses reported seeing cars lifted and hurled about like kindling, or as Myra Krenwitz, who lost her entire home but escaped without injury to herself or family, said, "Like Bugs in a fan!"

EDNA Lemme mute this thing. I can't hear you. (*she pops the remote*) You know where that is, that's nowhere near here. That's Texas I think. Or somewhere like that. Oh, I know, those poor people. That woman there—that poor woman, she lost everything. Poor things. (*pause*) I know, I meant to call you. I would have by tomorrow. I haven't been back home all that long. Oh, I had the greatest trip, it was the greatest visit. I just have the greatest kids. You know when I got my diagnosis, well, we didn't know which way to turn. We were looking for a place for me out east, because they're both in Massachusetts. Not that I could ever actually leave here to go live way out there. Been here all my life, don't you know. And anyway I been feeling so good, "Well," Andrew said, "either I'm putting the kids on a plane and we're all coming out to see you, or you're coming here for a visit." I didn't think I could do it. And I couldn't if they hadn't done everything for me. Jenny came and got me and flew out with me, and it was first class, I'll have you know. That's right. Andrew paid, and oh my, the room you have. I might just as well have been in this recliner where I'm sitting this second for the whole flight. It was a beautiful. A beautiful flight. Not a bump in the sky the whole time. That's right. And then Andrew flew back with me—got me here and then he had to go on to Omaha then Los Angeles for business; that's where he's coming in from today. That's right, he's going to come for a visit. He should have got into Chicago hours ago, and so he should be landing here any minute. If the damn thing's on time. It was first class with him, too. First class both ways. Like I was a queen. And the service? Well, they're just there every minute with "Can I get you this and can I get you that?" We had a full meal. The poor people back in coach, they're packed in like eggs in a crate and I don't think they get even a sandwich anymore. No. I never did before. First time in my life. And it's a good thing, too, because it spoils you. Jenny said, "I don't think I can fly any other way, after this, Mom." (*pause*) Yes. Beautiful birthday I had. A wonderful party at each of their houses. First I had the one at Andrew's and then when I went to Jenny's house, I had another one.

And do you know what they had for me at Andrew's? Oh, the kids were so sweet. And on the cake, this candle that when you lit it, it sang happy birthday. No. The candle. That's what I'm saying. It sang this little tune when you lit it. I know. What'll they think of next? It did me a lot of good. More than anybody knows. And do you know what? All of a sudden, I'm worried tyin' up this phone. (*moving downstage she looks out, as if through a large window*) What if Andrew's trying to call from the airport if something went wrong? You know those damn little planes coming into this one-horse town—Oh! (*startled looking off*) There's a cab pulling up in the courtyard. I bet that's him. Yes, yes, it is. (*hurrying back to the table*) I'll call you tomorrow. Bye.

She hangs up the phone and then Andrew enters. He's in his fifties and he carries a suitcase, and has a fairly large satchel over his shoulder. He carries a computer bag.

ANDREW   Hi, Mom.

EDNA   How was the flight?

ANDREW   Okay. You know. Not bad. Good to see you, Mommy. (*bending to hug and kiss her*)

EDNA   You don't know what a treat it is to see you walk in that door.

He sets the suitcase down and takes the satchel off.

ANDREW   I'm going to have a little drink, okay. Before I unpack.

EDNA   I don't know what I got here for you.

ANDREW   You stay put. I brought something.

With a pint of Jack Daniels taken from his suitcase, he goes to the kitchen for a glass, some ice from the refrigerator.

When I was leaving LA, the plane sat on the runway for over an hour. Just sat there.

EDNA   Oh, you must be exhausted. Why'd they do that?

ANDREW I think because they didn't have the pilot aboard. We were waiting for the pilot.

EDNA Oh, goodness, can't go without him.

ANDREW We sure didn't. (*walking downstage, he addresses the audience*) You just sit, right. And it's hot, because they can't keep the air-conditioning going, and, you're stuck in this one position, and there was a girl in the seat across from me, and she was maybe twenty-five or so, maybe twenty-eight, and attractive in a very simple—I don't know—real way—a natural real way—not glamorous, but— And anyway, she started to get more and more uncomfortable. She stroked her arm with her fingers, tickling herself sort of to console herself, and then she started to twist around and sort of writhe with discomfort, like she could barely stand what was happening to her and it was very erotic after a while, the way she would stroke her arm, and then twist, and her hair would fall across her face, because she was twisting the way people do sometimes when they're just on the verge of orgasm and they can hardly stand it. (*pivoting back to Edna*) Anyway, I made it.

EDNA I been telling everybody what a wonderful trip I had. Oh, I just keep thinking about it all.

ANDREW I'm going to pull that other chair over.

He sets down his drink on a little table beside the one recliner and goes to the recliner against the wall.

EDNA Sure. Jenny does that too. Lugs it over as soon as she gets here, and then shoves it back when it's time to go. I don't like it sittin' there next to me empty, you know, when I'm here alone. Makes me feel lonely. Nobody in it. When Daddy was alive, these two chairs were always here side by side, as you well know.

He drags it over so it is adjacent to the other recliner, the table between them.

ANDREW I remember.

EDNA This was how we sat. He was in one, I was in the other. I just hate havin' it sit there empty.

ANDREW (*sitting down*)   Well, I'll be in it now.

EDNA   You hear people talk about whirlwind trips and now I had one—I'm all the way out east and then back here, and now you're here. Oh, I just keep thinking about it all.

ACTOR ONE (*with a cable she waves over her head*)   Andrew, she's got me on mute. I'm sorry I'm on mute. I bet you wish I wasn't on mute, don't you, Andrew.

ANDREW (*to Edna*)   Were you watching something, Mom?

EDNA   Think I'll turn it off. Okay? (*as Edna uses the remote*)

ACTOR ONE   Noooo.

ANDREW   Sure.

EDNA   I was just watchin' the news. Terrible tornado down south. Texas, I think. Are you hungry? I'd like you to eat a good warm meal.

ANDREW   I'm okay.

EDNA (*crossing toward the kitchen*)   Not that I could fix it for you with all your food peculiarities. But maybe I can before you go, maybe I can cook you a meal, if you want. What would you like? I could make a meat loaf—remember I did that for your last trip, didn't I?

ANDREW   Yeh, it was good, too.

EDNA   Hard to hold it together without bread crumbs, though.

ANDREW   Well, they're not good for me, you know. I mean, bread crumbs. It's other normal stuff too, like fruit even and vinegar.

EDNA   I don't understand that.

ANDREW   Me neither.

EDNA   My blood sugar's been real good lately. I mean, I take enough pills for a small army of wounded soldiers, but so what? So far, so good. Knock on wood. These Lasix that I take for my heart, to drain the fluid, do you know how much they cost. Five dollars a pill. And

13

with those other ones—well I might as well throw money out the window. How you been doin' with that food mess of yours, okay?

ANDREW   I started taking these digestive enzymes and they're helping.

EDNA   Oh, yeh, you said that. I remember. Can you travel with them?

ANDREW   Sure, they're just little pills.

EDNA   (*grabbing her checkbook from off the kitchen table, she takes it to him*)   That's good. You know I do have a few things I'd like you to do for me. Maybe we could run over to the bank and have them straighten out my checking account, because I just can't make the darn thing balance.

ANDREW   I'll take a look at it.

EDNA   Their statement say I got a hundred dollars less than my own checkbook says. That's nothing to sneeze at.

ANDREW   It sure isn't.

As he takes the checkbook, she hurries back to the kitchen table, pulling photographs and a toy whale from a bag.

EDNA   And I want you to help me put out the new pictures of your kids. I want them where people will see them when they come in. And Nicky's little whale. I want to hang it somehow. It was so sweet of him, the way he came in with that little whale for me and he brought it in and said, "I brought you a present grandma." And then fixed it up like this—(*demonstrating how the whale hangs from a ribbon*) one of those—what do you call them? You hang them?

ANDREW   Mobile.

EDNA   Is that it?

ANDREW   Yeh.

EDNA   Oh, yeh. And another thing, at some point I want to go over all the pictures I have here, all the old photographs of my family and you kids growing up and I want you to take what you want. Pick some to take home.

ANDREW Okay.

EDNA Because to tell the truth I don't want them around anymore. I want to get rid of them.

ANDREW You do?

EDNA Yes, I do. They make me too darn sad.

ANDREW Really?

EDNA Yep. Really. (*pause*) How are the dogs?

ANDREW (*crossing to her at the table*) You mean all those photograph albums you've been collecting over the years, that you've been taking such good care of and all the pictures you saved and we sent you?

EDNA That's right.

ANDREW But Mom, how can you want to get rid of them?

EDNA I just told you, they make me too darn sad.

ANDREW Wow.

Brief silence.

EDNA Anywho . . .

ANDREW Okay. I guess.

EDNA And the videos, too.

ANDREW What? The videos, too? All those videos I took and copied and sent to you?

EDNA Same thing. (*as she heads for the VHS tapes piled up near the TV stand*) I just can't watch 'em. It hurts.

ANDREW But I thought you loved them.

EDNA Don't get me wrong, when you sent them out here, we loved them. Dad and me. Gettin' to see the kids at different ages, their birthday parties and things like that. Not the same as havin' 'em next door or in the same town, even. No substitute for the real thing. But it was wonderful that you did all that for us and sent them, and dad and me we watched them over and over. But it's different now. That's all. It's all just different.

The cuckoo goes off, the bird popping in and out five times.

ANDREW   He's going to keep doing that, isn't he.

EDNA   After you worked so hard gettin' him fixed last time you were out here, you bet he is.

ANDREW   I'm going to rig him so he doesn't, okay.

Andrew adjusts the two weights hanging down from the little house, as Edna drifts toward him.

EDNA   I like it when I'm here alone, but we can give him a little rest. Reminds me of my dad, you know, and all the care he took makin' it. Hand carved, you know, every leaf and feather. Sometimes I forget myself, but it's a thing of beauty.

ANDREW   (*back in his chair he looks at her up by the clock.*)   The dogs are good. But Drava had diarrhea, did I tell you?

EDNA   No. (*returning to her recliner*)

ANDREW   I heard her yapping to get out in the middle of the night, and I let her out at maybe two in the morning. I didn't realize what was going on. I thought she was just being fussy. I was mad at her.

EDNA   The poor thing; she was trying to tell you.

ANDREW   I know, but it was the middle of the night.

EDNA   You don't think right then.

ANDREW   There was a lot to keep track of. I had to get to the airport to meet you and Jenny. And Angela was leaving for camp later that same morning.

EDNA She told me all about that. Where they live in cabins in the woods but do their studies anyway. Is that good for her, do you think?

ANDREW Oh, sure.

EDNA I loved those dogs. Just watchin' 'em, you know.

ANDREW Did you?

EDNA Oh, yeh, they got such ways about them. Especially that Drava. She's cunning.

ANDREW And Jade.

EDNA Oh that Jade—she's a special one—a special dog—such a sweetheart. I have to say it just tickled me the way they all come troopin' up to my room when I was gettin' ready to leave. I'm packin' my suitcase and in they come. All four of 'em. And that Jade, she just plops down on the bed where I'm sittin' to catch my breath and she wouldn't take her eyes off me. I swear. It was like she knew I was leavin' and she wouldn't be seeing much more of me, and she wanted to get her fill. I tell you it gimme such a nice feeling. Special. You know. And the other three, too, keepin' close watch. Smart, isn't it? They see a suitcase and know you're leavin'. I'm kinda like that when it comes to suitcases.

ANDREW Sure.

Silence. Andrew takes the final sip of his drink.

EDNA Well, look at us blabbin' away when I bet what you want is to get settled in your room.

ANDREW That's probably a good idea. Then I can relax.

Andrew moves to take his suitcase into the room, crossing in front of Actor Two who has ended up watching all this from up near the bathroom door.

ACTOR TWO Isn't it odd? Almost shocking. (*crossing toward the audience*) They don't even mention me. And I'm the reason he's

17

here for this visit. They just saw each other, and there have been times when years passed without a visit. But I'm here now and my appetite—my appetite is shameless—and unrelenting—for her body that I want to overtake and devour.

Andrew goes in and out of the room, getting his jacket, picking up the satchel.

EDNA   You need me to give you a hand with anything?

ANDREW   No, I don't think so.

ACTOR TWO   There was a little flaw in her. Partly nutritional, partly time with its wear and tear, and partly— Well I won't say. I have my secrets. I took advantage. I won't say of what. I need my secrets. Meant to die, I refused. Who wouldn't if they could? I found a way to replicate—to slip my intrinsic doom—to defy my nature. I veil myself as friendly, so that I can insinuate, infiltrate, cloaked and unidentifiable as who I really am. I move among the innocent and dutiful of my former kind and I flourish upon a bright and tidal foam of appetite and self self self perpetuation, and now, unlike my dull, obedient, and subservient brethren, I have become immortal.

EDNA   And do you have any calls to make, Andrew? People you want to get in touch with? What about Sam and Sally? Or Ronny? You should call them. You boys were the best friends. I want you to do some things you enjoy, while you're here. And Maggie Hull always wants to see you. She'd be hurt if you didn't at least give her a call.

ANDREW   I'm here to see you Mom, this time.

EDNA   You gotta call Maggie. She's so good to me. I tell you. Always thinking about me. Calling and stopping by. Asking what I need or if she can do something for me. It's even more now since Tessa died. With her Mom gone, I think Maggie thinks of me as sort of a substitute, you know.

ANDREW   Sure.

EDNA I get lonely, both of you kids out east the way you are, and then Maggie pops by or calls. And it lifts the cloud.

ANDREW (*finished now, he comes out*) I just don't want to make too many dates and then not have enough time with you. (*flopping down in the recliner*)

EDNA Don't you worry about that. We'll have our time. I'll see to it.

ANDREW Okay.

Taking a crocheted blanket from the back of a kitchen chair, Edna carries it into Andrew's room.

EDNA You can't just come in and out of town like you're a thief on the run, you know. People hear about it, and their feelings get hurt. And then I gotta make excuses.

With Edna gone, Actor Two eyes Andrew.

ACTOR TWO You look tired, Andrew. Stressed and worried. Secretive. Like me, you're deeply hidden. Even from yourself, as you so often feel and know. I am despised and called malignant, but I view myself quite differently. It's a masquerade, a game of espionage. In the shadows. Survival at stake. Mine is what I desire. I'd like you, too, Andrew. I'll take you, too, if I get the chance. You have your flaws, I'm sure. So worried and stressed. I wish you still smoked. But . . . well . . . we'll see.

Scene ii

Lights fade to black and distant thunder rumbles; rain begins.

When lights rise it's later that evening with Edna at the table. Andrew sits in his recliner with the local paper. Edna picks up the vase of flowers and moves toward Andrew.

EDNA Can I bother you about somethin'?

ANDREW Sure.

19

EDNA Take a little sniff? They're startin' to get droopy and they don't exactly stink but they're not exactly fresh. I'm thinkin' I ought to throw them out. But they're kind of pretty yet.

ANDREW I think they're okay.

EDNA They don't smell bad to you? (*taking another sniff*) I guess not. Let 'em hang on a bit more. Poor things.

On the way back to the table, she looks out at the ongoing rain.

That darn rain. Doesn't sound like it's going to let up.

ANDREW Paper says it's supposed to.

EDNA (*irritated at the weather foiling plans*) I was hoping we might get up to the cemetery tomorrow and visit Dad's grave. Maybe stop by Grandpa and Grandma's grave, too.

ANDREW We still might be able to.

EDNA It'll be wet.

ANDREW It'll probably stop soon.

EDNA But it'll be wet. (*crossing back to sit and crochet*) I get up there as often as I can. I don't like it to get run-down the way I see some graves when they go too long without somebody looking after them. It looks too sad, you know.

ANDREW Mmmhmmm.

EDNA Like nobody cares.

ANDREW We'll be sure to get up there before I go.

He turns a page, then glances at the TV. Actor One waves at him.

ACTOR ONE Andrew. I have an idea. If you don't want to have to talk about graveyards and grave stones, there's three hundred and twenty-two channels. Check out the guide. You can find something, I promise.

ANDREW You wanna watch some TV, Mom?

EDNA   Oh, I don't know. Not just now I don't think.

ACTOR ONE   There's *Tom and Jerry, Full House. Happy Days.* And *Seinfeld. Seinfeld* is barely started.

EDNA   Are you thinking you'd like to turn it on?

ANDREW   I don't know. Sort of.

ACTOR ONE   On *Seinfeld* George buys an arcade game to preserve his high score, and fear of a serial killer puts a dent in Jerry's social life.

EDNA   Go ahead if you want.

ACTOR ONE   There's a three-star old movie. *The Plainsman and the Lady.* And *Perfect Strangers* is coming up! While out shopping for presents, Balki and Cousin Larry get locked in the department store with a big dog.

EDNA   Truth to tell, I'd just as soon leave it off. Unless there's somethin' you're really itchin' to watch.

ANDREW   No, not really.

ACTOR ONE   But it's funny—what happens to Balki and Larry. You get that. The big dog is scary and their fear is funny.

Andrew goes back to the newspaper, while Edna crochets.

EDNA   At least we can be thankful it wasn't pourin' cats and dogs when you had to fly in. Rain and wind and wind shear. You read about that stuff. What is wind shear, anyway?

ANDREW   I don't really know.

EDNA   You read about it all the time.

ANDREW   I think it does something to the way the plane stays up in the air. The wings, by moving forward, create this updraft, right?

EDNA   I have no idea.

ANDREW   Or something. It has something to do with updraft, or something like that, and it's mathematical in as far as the weight of

21

the plane with whatever is on board has to be matched by . . . or compensated for by the size of the wing and the speed of the plane. And wind shear messes that up—that equation, and so the plane could plummet.

EDNA   Is that a fact.

ANDREW   That may not be exactly right, but it's pretty close.

He goes back to reading while she continues to crochet.

EDNA   You know I just keep wondering if that darn Dr. Grennel should have made me do a Pap smear and pelvic exam. So we coulda got a head start on this thing. Caught it before it got so far along. Mindy says Grennel is no damn good. I can't go along with that completely, because I think he saved my life with the colostomy operation, but he let me down. When I say I might ask him why nobody at that dang HMO had the good sense to give me a Pap smear and mammogram, well, Mindy says they will just tell me, "Well, you didn't ask for them." Like I'm supposed to know.

ANDREW   That doesn't seem right. They must have given you a physical.

EDNA   Somewhere along the line, sure, but they got these guidelines. Fifteen minutes a visit and a physical every six months.

ANDREW   What I'm thinking Mom is it's probably not Grennel, as much as his bosses, the bureaucrats, the bean counters who set the guidelines.

EDNA   All those doctors down there are the bosses, Andrew. They own that HMO. And Grennel's the president. He's a big shot. And you know he never even talked about sending me down to Iowa City for the specialists there to take a look at me. It's like I wasn't worth the bother. I can't help feelin' he gave up on me. I'm old. So they figure I'm ready for the scrap heap. Well, the heck with that noise. It's just a big disappointment you know. I thought I could count on him. And now I'm in this pickle. Like a rat in a trap. I hope it's a Havahart trap, you know what I mean.

ANDREW   Sure.

EDNA   I hope it's one of those traps that takes the mouse prisoner, and then you go somewhere and let him loose. You ever use one of them things?

ANDREW   Sure. We used to take the prisoner out into the woods.

EDNA   In the old days we only had those that came down on their neck. Poor things are tryin' to get a bite of cheese, next thing they know, they're dead. Except this one—I went to pick him up and he blinked at me. Scared the bejeezus out of me. And then he run off. I guess that's a happy story.

ANDREW   You got any snacks? Or maybe I should run over to Eagles and pick some stuff up.

EDNA   There's Ritz crackers. And some potato chips. In the cabinet by the sink. Want me to get them?

ANDREW   No, I can do it. (*moving into the kitchen*) I'm going to have some milk, too.

EDNA   Help yourself. You know . . . Andrew!

ANDREW   What's that, Mom?

EDNA   That doctor in Boston, the really special one you had look at my X-rays. You think a lot of him, right?

ANDREW   Oh, I sure do, Dr. Sebastian is one of the top oncologists on the whole east coast.

EDNA   And I guess we'd have to say he didn't see much to give us any hope, did he? When he looked at my X-rays. I'm tryin' to remember what he said. What was it again?

As Andrew in the kitchen gathers crackers on a plate and milk.

ANDREW   I told you what he said, Mom.

EDNA   But it was just kind of odd the way he put it, I thought. I was hoping—I guess we all were, that people in Boston might know better than out here, have some kind of better idea what to do.

ANDREW   We were all hoping that, Mom.

EDNA   But what was that funny thing he said?

ANDREW   What funny thing?

EDNA   You know. That word. He had a word you wouldn't expect about a person like me. I think about it sometimes and I want to have it right. What I'm thinking. The word he used. (*beat*) How'd he put it again?

ANDREW   Well, he said . . . if I remember right. It's a while back, but . . .

EDNA   This was after he looked at all the X-rays, right?.

ANDREW   (*still fussing in the kitchen*)   Yes. He had them all, and he was looking at one of the very early ones and one of the last couple, and he said there was a "shadow." I think was the word.

EDNA   No, that's not it. Not the one I'm tryin' to get.

ANDREW   (*annoyed at being forced to render the details again*)   He said there was a shadow, and it was a kind of destiny. That there was a kind of "destiny" in the X-rays. Between the early one and the late one, there was a kind of destiny. Is that what you mean?

EDNA   You know, if we get up to that darn cemetery, when we go, we need to take something to dig with. I have one of those claws. But I don't know if it would be enough. Maybe I should bring a knife.

ANDREW   Whatever you think.

Crossing back, he picks up the remote.

EDNA   If it's too wet, I maybe won't go down to Daddy's grave. I'll just go to Mom and Dad. Grandma and Grandpa. Their grave is closer to the road and I can make a little visit.

24

Andrew aims the remote and turns on the TV.

ACTOR ONE   Blondes! Brunettes! Tall beautiful girls with long hair all bright and beaming:

Seeing that it's a commercial, Andrew starts back to the kitchen where he left his snacks. Passing behind Edna's chair, he catches sight of her, gazing off in distress. He moves a few steps more as the TV rattles on, and then he stops and watches Edna. As the commercial nears its end, he moves to stand behind Edna.

"JAN MARINI Revitalizing Conditioner turns tired, dry, or chemically damaged hair into lush, full, and younger-looking hair!" Look at the blonde! Look at the brunette! Both brilliant, aglow. "Thinning, aging hair is revitalized into the hair of your dreams with renewed body and bounce!" With life, vitality, vivaciousness!

ANDREW (*leaning close*)   I want to do that, Mommy.

EDNA   What?

ANDREW (*his baby talk is an awkward offer of closeness after snapping at her*)   I want to weevitawize my haiwww . . .

EDNA   Pawdon me?

ANDREW   I want to wee vita wize my haiwww.

EDNA   What?

ACTOR ONE   Re vitalize.

ANDREW   I want to RE-vitalize my hiawr

EDNA   Oh, oh. RE vitalize. That's what I need. A little something to revitalize me head to toe.

ANDREW   They were talking about it on the TV. I want to weee-vita—wize my haiwww.

EDNA   Sounds fine to me. Somebody oughta weeevitawize not only my haiw but my everything!

ACTOR ONE   It's JAN MARINI Revitalizing Conditioner that turns tired hair new.

EDNA   So I guess you're gonna watch a little TV.

ANDREW   I don't have to.

ACTOR ONE   Don't mute me. C'mon.

Andrew pops the mute button.

EDNA   It's okay. You go ahead. I'm about ready to drop, tryin' to stay up with you like there's no tomorrow, or you won't be here tomorrow. When you will. But I just gotta give in before I pass out. I got lots of cleanin' up. That darn colostemy bag. Ewwwww. I hate it.

ANDREW   But it's good, too, right? I mean, what it does for you.

EDNA   No two ways about that. I thank my lucky stars. That operation got me just in time, otherwise it's peritonitis and curtains for me. I just wish they coulda reversed the darn business.

ANDREW   I remember when you woke up in the hospital bed, it was your first question and you were so darn disappointed they couldn't reverse it.

EDNA   Too much scar tissue. (*rising*) Anyway, I gotta do my teeth and whatnot. And say my prayers. I got these nice prayers.

ANDREW   Oh, yeah.

EDNA   Good ones, you know. One to to St Perigrine. And another one the Blessed Mother. Never known to fail, they say.

Moving to go, she drifts to the big window looking out on the night and rain.

I don't know for sure, but it does make me feel better. Closer to her, you know. Somebody out there in that big black night . . . and that darn rain—somebody out there cares.

Actor Two enters into the kitchen and stands close by, as Andrew goes back to the newspaper, and Edna sensing Actor Two looks at him. Then,

26

turning to hurry to her room, she yelps fearfully at the sight of Andrew in the chair.

Oh, that gimme a start. I halfway forgot you were here, and then seein' you in that chair mixed me up with Daddy sittin' there, the way he would, wantin' to stay up watchin' movies. Sports. What have you. Till all hours of the night.

ANDREW   I know.

EDNA   Even after the accident. The man was a night owl. I'd sit up as long as I could, or he'd have to call me because he couldn't get to bed on his own. Do you ever think what it musta been like for him trapped in that car the way he was? His neck broke. (*growing increasingly angry*) He can't move. He's out on that lonely road all by himself in the dark. Miles from nowhere. What that musta been like.

ANDREW   I know.

EDNA (*a little angry at Andrew*)   Do you ever think about it? Sometimes I just wanna run out and help the poor guy, like he's still there. And sometimes I wake up and see him here. (*looking at Actor Two who starts to walk*) Yes, I do. Look at me like I'm crazy if you want. I see him shufflin' around the apartment with his walker. Those little steps he had to take. That big strong man. Those braces on his wrists. (*watching Actor Two exit*)

ANDREW   You actually think you see him?

EDNA   I'm usually half asleep. Just waking up, or something.

ANDREW   And you see him?

EDNA   You know that dream I told you about that's just been haunting me. (*agitated, pacing*)

ANDREW   Sure. You mean the one where you got locked out of the apartment.

EDNA   That's the one. Well, I was on the phone with Jenny the other morning and I told her, and she said, "Well, mom that dream is just so real I can just tell you what it is. You been saying you feel so all alone. Okay," she said. "Daddy died first. Then Tessa, your best friend—your life-long friend died, and there you are standin' out in the cold. Locked out of your home." Now isn't that Jenny something? She thinks she's got my dream all analyzed.

Andrew shakes his head, chuckles.

Yeah! See you don't believe it, huh.

ANDREW   No, no, I thought of that.

EDNA   Did you really? I wish you'da told me.

ANDREW   Yeah. When you told me, I—I—

EDNA (*every detail emphatic*)   It was the very day Tessa was gonna be laid out down at Gears funeral parlor that I had it. Do you remember that? I was so antsy all that day and I just had to get out of the apartment. I was so—I just had no rest—so I took myself out to the mall all by myself and walked around and went to evening mass and came home and fell asleep. And then . . . it was clear as day—Tessa and me were outside and Daddy left first and took the car and went down to Gears funeral parlor where Tessa was going to be laid out that very night. And all of a sudden she went, too. And I tried to get back in the apartment, but I'd locked myself out. I got so hysterical, because I was all alone out in the cold and I couldn't get back in here. I woke myself up. I was all wrapped up in the covers. It's haunting me still, if you know what I mean.

ANDREW   It's a very powerful dream, Mom.

EDNA   Yes, it is! And I could see it so clear. (*emphasizing each detail to make clear its importance*) I didn't see much of Daddy. He just went out real fast and got in his car and went with his coat on. A winter coat. His topcoat. And Tessa was all bundled up and we were out in the courtyard talking, and then she left, too, and I stood out there, trying to get myself back into the house. And you know when I think about it, maybe it does mean that.

ANDREW   Well, mom, you know if you look at it that way, it's almost literal.

EDNA   It just made me think the whole rest of that day . . .

ANDREW   About what? Exactly.

EDNA   That maybe it did mean that I'm lonely. I'd been saying that I feel so alone without Tessa and Daddy.

ANDREW   And they were both going to Gears.

EDNA   That's right, and I knew that, and I wasn't very happy to be going there, because I don't like the way fix their people down there. *(sitting back in the recliner next to Andrew)*

ANDREW   What do they do?

EDNA   They just—they don't do like Rymans Sauter fixed Daddy. You know, he looked awful when he died, and the way they fixed him, I thought he looked wonderful, and everybody says that about Rymans Sauter. But Gears don't even have them laying down right. They have them sit up; they have their heads cocked up funny . . . in the casket. And don't you know, they have almost every funeral in town. Rymans Sauter is getting nothing. Because Gears does it so cheap and he turns them out like on a—what would you say? You know what I'm tryin' to say.

ANDREW   Assembly line?

EDNA   Yeah. Just about like that. I've been there so many times for women from work, and I haven't seen one yet that looked like they should. I remember telling the lady who took me to church that day—we were in her car, and she said, "Where's Tessa going to be?" and I said "Gears," and she said, "Oh, god no." I said, "Yeah." They just do awful work, if you want to call it work. So anyway . . . it doesn't matter, I guess. Daddy's been gone a long time. And now Tessa's gone maybe three months. And it gets me. I just get so depressed sometimes . . . feelin' all alone. I'll be all right, though. *(rising, she heads for her room)* Anyway, 'night now. And this time I mean it.

29

ANDREW   'Night mom. See you in the morning.

EDNA   See you in the morning. Don't that sound nice.

She closes the door to her room and Andrew begins channel-hopping pointing with the remote.

ACTOR ONE   "—we can't know what they're planning. It's not possible without more informa—" (*hop*) "—These Cub pitchers have got to stop all these self-inflicted wounds; they just shoot themselves in the foot. A walk here will—" (*hop*) "—please listen to me. I know I was wrong, but—" (*hop*) "—the Best in Beauty towlette tells your facial lines where to go. Give your face—" (*hop*) With this yogurt, if you were any more satisfied, you'd blush."

Lights go out on Andrew and Actor One and rise on Edna seated on the edge of her bed ready to pray. Actor Two appears and stands near the head board.

EDNA   Prayer to the Blessed Mother. Oh, most beautiful flower of Mount Carmel, Fruitful Vine, Splendor of Heaven, Immaculate Virgin, Blessed Mother of the Son of God— Oh show me herein you are my Mother. There is none that can withstand your power.

ACTOR TWO   It's like a little poem. So soothing. Almost sweet. Hopeful. Sad. Innocent.

EDNA   Oh Holy Mary, Mother of God, Queen of Heaven and Earth—I humbly beseech thee from the bottom of my heart to help me in this my necessity.

ACTOR TWO   Edna, I feel nothing. If it's meant to trouble me, I don't feel it.

EDNA   O Star of the Sea—Help me and show me herein you are my Mother. Please help me heal from this sickness. O Mary, conceived without sin, pray for us. Pray for us who have recourse to thee. Sweet Mother, I place this cause in your hands. Amen.

ACTOR TWO   Amen.

Slowly, Edna lies back. He stays looking down at her.

That's right, Edna, my one and only. You need to rest. You have too many worries. But now Andrew is here, and you can put your worries aside at last. What's your favorite memory among all those you love from when he was small? Those little toy pistols and those little toy holsters? Those cowboy movies he loved? Just two years ago you sent him a birthday card that said . . .

EDNA   Happy Birthday to my cowboy. Love and prayers. Mom.

ACTOR TWO   So stop worrying. He probably doesn't care that you actually said out loud that you see his dead father walking around.

EDNA   Why couldn't I keep my big trap shut? I could just kick myself. He probably thinks I'm ready for the loony bin.

ACTOR TWO   Edna, it's all right.

EDNA   I don't know why it just come out of me.

ACTOR TWO   You shouldn't have said it, but you did and now it's too late to take it back. There's no point in trying to or wishing you could. So stop. The night is long and deep and dark and you're alone in it. But I'll be with you. Close by. What did you want from him, telling him that? Do you even know?

EDNA   I gotta get some rest.

ACTOR TWO (*intimate, even consoling*)   I think you were hoping to take something yours alone, almost secret and precious, and share it with him.

EDNA (*ridiculous*)   No, no, no.

ACTOR TWO   You have so much to worry about that you can't worry about it all. It's impossible.

EDNA   I know. I gotta stop. Okay? Please let me sleep.

ACTOR TWO   I'm weary, too. I'm exhausted, too.

EDNA   Okay then. (*lying back, patting his hand, which rests on the headboard*) Let's get some rest. (*she settles, then bolts up*) You're lying. You're up to no good. Plotting and conniving every second. I don't dare turn my back. Admit it.

ACTOR TWO   Edna, please. You'll never understand my strategies. My counterstrategies. My counter-counterstrategies. My secret allies who lurk in your depths, the dark, your very core, where everything is hidden, their name and natures unknown. Now good night.

   BLACKOUT

Scene iii

   Edna enters from her bedroom, carrying one of the photograph albums, which she puts down on the kitchen table where the other album waits. As she moves to the refrigerator, the front door opens and Andrew comes in carrying a bag of groceries.

EDNA   Get everything?

ANDREW   I think so.

EDNA   Find everything you need, all that yogurt?

ANDREW   Yep. And do you know, I think I have that checkbook thing figured out. You made a little mistake subtracting.

EDNA   Is that what happened? Can you show me?

ANDREW   You subtracted sixty-eight when it should have been one hundred sixty-eight. (*as he hands her the checkbook, she sits down at the table*)

EDNA   What? Why the heck would I do that?

ANDREW (*pointing to the open checkbook*)   Right here. You came up with one hundred forty-four when it's just forty-four.

EDNA (*studying intently*)   Andrew. No. Twelve minus eight is four and then if you—

32

ANDREW (*moving back to the groceries*)   But, Mom, you're skipping the one there.

EDNA   I don't see any one. Where's this one you keep talking about?

ANDREW   It's right there. So it ends up a hundred dollars off.

EDNA   Where? (*she studies*) Oh, now, don't you see? Look at that. That darn one looks like it's a line in the box—a part of the box. I mistook it. They give you so little room to write in. Just these little bitty boxes. It's like they want you to feel like a dummy. Daddy used to do all the addin' and subtractin', don't you know, always keepin' track for the both of us. He loved doin' it, and oh my, especially when that monthly check arrived in the mailbox from you. I'd bring it in and let him open it, because I knew how he enjoyed it, and he'd look at that check and then he'd nod and gimme a look. I'd bring him over the checkbook so he could add it in as a deposit. Then I'd take it over to the bank the next morning. That's the way we did it.

ANDREW   It wasn't that much, Mom. (*preparing a snack of yogurt*)

EDNA   It was plenty and we couldn't have done without it. It made all the difference. We had our social security, the both of us, and some savings, but that check was what gave us just that little extra. But I messed it up good now. I guess I better go back and do it all over.

ANDREW   I don't think you have to go that far. If we just add it up and put the correct number at the end, you can go on. (*crossing to the recliner*)

EDNA   I want to have it right, so when you're not around to check, I can make sure they're not cheatin' me over there.

ANDREW   I don't think they're cheatin' you at the bank, mom. (*seated in the recliner, ready to relax*)

EDNA   You never know. You hear about that kind of thing all the time. Somebody—not necessarily some bigwig, but maybe just this little nobody, low on the totem pole, a loose cannon, but clever. So he's figurin' "That old fool'll never catch on." Not that he'd squeeze much out of me but if he pulled the same stunt on a bunch of old people he could rake in a pretty penny.

ANDREW You made a mistake, Mom. Nobody's cheating you.

Briefly Edna fiddles at the table with the photo albums.

EDNA So I guess if you got nothin' better to do, now might be the time to look over the photo albums. Like I mentioned yesterday.

ANDREW Okay.

EDNA I got 'em all set up here.

ANDREW I see that.

EDNA So maybe you leaf through and see what you might want to take.

ANDREW (*crossing to the table*) I can't believe you really mean this.

EDNA Well, I do. Why did I ever keep these things? They just make me sad. That's what I keep telling you. There's no way around it.

ANDREW (*standing behind her, looking*) Whata you got there?

EDNA Picnic up at the park with that gang Dad come to town with, surveying for the damn. It's about when we first met.

ANDREW They look like a good bunch.

EDNA (*suddenly stricken*) Oh, Lord. Just look, will you? Look how beautiful I was. Look how I looked. And the way I look now. (*another page*) And ohh, Daddy. Look how beautiful Daddy was.

ANDREW See that's what I just don't understand.

EDNA Wasn't he though?

ANDREW He was very handsome. But why get rid of them then, if—

EDNA Andrew, how many times do I have to say it?

ANDREW   Okay. I mean, you know what you want, I guess, but—

EDNA   You have to take these off my hands, any you want, all right? You can show 'em to the kids. I can't have them here.

ANDREW   And then what? You'll throw the rest out?

As Edna continues, Andrew paces away; he picks up her cane near the door and starts to use it as a golf club, practicing his grip, his stroke.

EDNA   Yes. And we have to talk about the furniture. What to do with it all? It's not much, I know. But it's no easy matter, let me tell you. Jenny and I thought we'd figure it out. We were thinking maybe I'd shut the apartment up and move out east. But we went sort of crazy trying to decide what to do with everything. We had this woman come by, secondhand furniture person and we about drove her crazy, too. What should we do with the TV, the recliners, this nice table—it belonged to Grandma, you remember. And somebody's got to have Grandpa's cuckoo clock. *(looking at Andrew engaged with his golf swing)* What the heck are you doing with my cane, Andrew?

ANDREW   I'm listening.

EDNA   I sure hope so, but what are you doing?

ANDREW   Just practicing a little. This new golf swing I've been learning.

EDNA   Oh. Okay.

ANDREW   I have these video tapes from this instructor. It's a whole different approach.

EDNA   Just be careful. I gotta use that thing when I get that plantar fasciitus. And my knee comes and goes.

ANDREW   I won't hurt it.

EDNA   You better not.

ANDREW   Do you want me not to use it?

EDNA   No. You go ahead.

ANDREW   Most golf instructors talk about the swing being controlled by the lower body, by your thighs and shifting weight, and the hands just react and do what they're supposed to, which to me is nuts. It'd be like a dentist telling you he controls the drill with his thighs.

EDNA   Anyway, so you'll pick a few photos out to take home and then I can do what I want with the rest.

It's somewhat tense now.

ANDREW   Actually, Mom, I think I'll take them all. So . . . you maybe have to look through to see what you want to keep.

EDNA   I have what I want. All framed and up in my room, or there. (*indicating the wall*) Mainly your kids. Some of you and Jenny. And that's it. (*beat*) I'm sorry to put this on you kids, but I had to tell you when the diagnosis came in. We have to face it.

ANDREW   I know. I know. But you seem so good, though.

EDNA   I feel good. But you know what they told me at the HMO, and that darn oncologist wasn't very nice about it, either. He's a cold fish, that Wingert. Everybody says it.

They sit. Silence.

Did you hear that thunder last night?

ANDREW   Oh, yeah.

As before, their baby talk bridges their stiff.

EDNA   It was scawwwy. It was such big booms.

ANDREW   Vewwwy scewwwwy.

EDNA   I was so scawweeed that I pulled the covers up over my head. All da way owva.

ANDREW   I was so vewwy vewy scaweed I just wanted to stay in my bed. I didn't pull the covers up over my hewd, but I wanted towwww.

EDNA We better put a stop to this baby talk before we get arrested.

A little laughter.

ANDREW You know who I ran into when I was shopping? Sammy!

EDNA At our Eagles? What was he doin' down our way? Sale or something? There's a brand new Krogers up where him and Sally built their new house

ANDREW He didn't mention anything. But we were talking and golf came up, so he asked me to go over to the golf range with him tomorrow—the driving range after he gets off work. What do you think? Would that be all right?

EDNA That's what I've been telling you. You have to get out a little, before you go stir-crazy stuck here with me.

ANDREW You could come along if you wanted. (*rising with the cane*)

EDNA Me? What would I be doin'?

ANDREW There's a little shop, he says. You could have a cup of coffee or a diet soda and watch us out the window.

EDNA I don't think so.

ANDREW Might be fun, Mom. Get you out of the house.

EDNA It'll suit me just fine to hear about it. I love thinking of you out with Sam. (*on her way to her room*) You boys were such good friends growing up. No, you go ahead and have some fun.

ANDREW Okay then.

She watches Andrew take a practice swing.

EDNA Was that a good one?

ANDREW Maybe.

BLACKOUT

NIGHT. Actor Two sits in Andrew's recliner, while Actor One sits on the floor, holding a large TV antenna. She is bathed in the TV light.

ACTOR ONE   Vicky is stunned watching Chad go out the door to meet Jessica. Her eyes are disappointed; and then angry—they're furious—they're insane looking out the window at Chad walking to Jessica.

Edna comes out from her room in her robe, carrying a diet soda, watching the show intently as she sits with them.

Driving like a wild woman in her red convertible, Vicki is headed for trouble. The wind in her hair, that wanton look in her eye, she speeds around a corner high in the Hollywood Hills, the lights of Los Angeles bright below, and she swerves, squealing, bouncing off the curb, almost losing control, but laughing at the danger.

ACTOR TWO   That Vicki is such a devil.

EDNA   She sure is.

ACTOR TWO   She reminds me of your sister.

ACTOR ONE   Headlights race toward her and she honks crazily, over and over, as if the other car is in the wrong when it's Vicki who is driving out of control.

ACTOR TWO   I can't believe how much she's like Madeline. Neither one of them care a lick about anything or anybody, all the terrible damage they cause. Madeline was always trying to get away with something.

EDNA   Shush.

ACTOR TWO   What?

EDNA   I'm tryin' to watch the story. How can I watch the story with you yammerin' at me about this and that about my sister.

38

ACTOR TWO   I'm just saying . . . .

EDNA   I know what you're saying. I just don't want to think about Madeline right this second. She's gone to her maker, let the poor woman rest.

ACTOR TWO   She's gone to her maker mad as heck at you.

EDNA   I don't know that. (*engaged fully with him*)

ACTOR TWO   You know what she wrote in that last letter. That she was done with you forever. As far as she's concerned she no longer has a sister.

EDNA (*looking back to the TV*)   Now I missed half of what's goin' on, listenin' to you.

ACTOR ONE   Parking in the shadows, Vicki sneaks along the wall, slipping into the dimly lit driveway where the Mercedes is parked.

ACTOR TWO   Madeline was sneaky and nasty just like Vicki—I don't care what you say.

EDNA   I said you were right.

ACTOR TWO (*drawing her in*)   Why did she have to send you such a nasty, vicious letter? It's depressing, her saying that as far as she was concerned, she no longer had a sister.

EDNA   It hurt. I admit it.

ACTOR TWO   And then she dies. So that's the last thing you hear from her. Words from her death bed. From the grave almost.

EDNA   Will you shut up? (*completely fixated on Actor Two now*)

ACTOR TWO   That's what she leaves you with.

EDNA   I tole you I don't want to think about this stuff.

ACTOR ONE   Edna.

EDNA   What?

ACTOR ONE   Look at what Vicki's doing under Jessica's car. She's going to cut the brake line so that the next time Jessica drives, she will crash and die and Chad will be—

EDNA   You can just shut up, too.

ACTOR ONE   Why? What did I do?

Edna crosses toward the table where the photo albums still lie.

EDNA   We couldn't get along from day one almost. That's just the way it was. My very own sister. We rubbed each other wrong. Things would go along peachy for a while but then it would all go to the devil. One day she'd be all lovey dovey and the next ready to take your head off.

ACTOR TWO   Goodbye and good riddance.

EDNA   I don't feel that way.

ACTOR ONE   Edna? (*hurrying close, carrying the TV antenna*) If you don't want to watch *Evil Is As Evil Does*, maybe there's something else we can find.

EDNA   No, I don't want to.

ACTOR ONE   *The Bad News Bears* is on.

EDNA   Is it? That's a cute one.

ACTOR ONE   Or *Happy Days*. *Sanford and Son*. You need something to cheer you up, give you a good laugh.

ACTOR TWO   No, she does not. She's depressed. She's heartsick about her sister, and she's right to be. It makes you want to give up, doesn't it, Edna. And it should. It's a trap, and it's not a Havahart, but it's vicious. With teeth that make you feel hopeless. Because it is hopeless. Why don't you read Madeline's letter again? Just to remind yourself.

EDNA (*looking warily to the little desk in the kitchen*)   I don't know if that's such a good idea. It always kinda upsets me.

ACTOR TWO   But why not be upset? What's the point? No Tessa anymore. No Daddy. And a sister who hates you.

EDNA   It's a cryin' shame what went on between us.

ACTOR TWO (*advancing on Edna*)   You travel all the way to Cleveland to see her, because she had to move into assisted living. But there she is getting waited on hand and foot in this place; it might as well have been a big fancy hotel.

EDNA   Everything always had to be the best for Madeline. That was just her way. Her house, her car, her new dining set. Her husbands.

ACTOR TWO   And then you'd hardly been there a day when all the nitpicking started.

EDNA   Oh, boy did it ever. Pick, pick, pick.

ACTOR TWO   Pick, pick, pick. Your shoes were ugly, your skirt was boxy.

EDNA   What the heck, I'm boxy. I couldn't do anything to suit her. Not one thing. And once she got up a head of steam, there was no stoppin' her.

ACTOR TWO   You couldn't even walk to suit her. She says you walk funny. You need better shoes.

EDNA   I did my best to let it go in one ear and out the other, believe you me. She says she wants to give me some of her old clothes, but they would be too small. Because I'm fat—I should lose some weight. (*close to the desk now, but still hesitant*)

ACTOR TWO   And there she is, skin and bone, and with maybe half a lung, still smoking a pack a day.

EDNA   I told her, "I don't need your clothes, Maddy, I can buy my own clothes."

ACTOR TWO   But then she started runnin' Teddy down. That was the last straw.

EDNA You better believe it.

ACTOR TWO They never got along, Teddy and her. Not from the first second. He didn't kowtow to her, the way her husbands did.

EDNA No. He did not take her guff. Next thing I know she's telling me Teddy didn't treat me right. He didn't light my cigarette for me when I used to smoke. He didn't open the car door for me the way Biff did for her. Ohh, I can see that poor Biff, runnin' around like a trained seal. I don't care about those things, I told her. (*opening the drawer, taking out the envelope*)

ACTOR TWO But she just kept at it.

EDNA And Teddy's not there to defend himself. It ain't right.

ACTOR TWO The poor man is dead and gone.

EDNA "Let the poor man rest," I told her. I wasn't going to stand for it. Maybe he wasn't her kinda man, but he was mine. Ohh, she got into a huff. Nothin' but ice between us from that second on. I left a day or two later. Made some excuse. I don't know what. I wasn't home a week when I found this letter in my mail. She attacks me like you wouldn't believe—goin' way back to dredge up things I did to hurt her. All these little things—makin' mountains out of mole hills. But that's what she did. The both of us. Isn't that something, though. Two sisters, the pair of us on our last legs and that's what has to happen.

ACTOR TWO It's tragic and hopeless. I don't know how you can stand it.

EDNA I can't barely stand it. (*putting the letter away and picking up*) Because do you know what? All I want right this second is to pick up that phone and call her. All I can think of is good times when we were little, or when we used to sing together, called ourselves the *Doodle Dop Sisters*. We traveled around the whole state, don't you know, and got paid for it, too. I want to reminisce just once more. Have a nice visit. Pick up the phone and harmonize a little, even. It's a knife in my heart knowin' there's no fixin' it ever now. (*hanging up the phone*)

ACTOR ONE   Edna. Look at me. You really need to watch something.

ACTOR TWO   She's fine. We're doing fine.

ACTOR ONE   Edna, come on. Anything to change the mood.

EDNA   Maybe. Maybe you're right.

ACTOR TWO   But she's not, and you know it.

ACTOR ONE   I bet we can find a really really funny one. Just silly. Maybe even a *Golden Girls*. Wouldn't that be—

EDNA   No. No. Watchin' them *Golden Girls* will just makes me miss Tessa. I haven't looked at them darn fools since I lost her. The fun we used to have—her on the phone at her house and me on the phone here, the both of us watchin' and laughin', and we looked forward to that darn *Frasier*, too. But we couldn't do none of that, she got so sick. I didn't have her for the whole last six months, and now I'll never have her again. Friends for all those years. Got married on the same day, Tessa and Ray, and me and Teddy, and then we met on the train, the Zepher takin' us to Chicago for our honeymoons. Neither of us had any money to speak of. So we did things together. Friends ever since.

ACTOR ONE   How about a love story then, like you and Teddy and Ray and Tessa meeting on that train?

EDNA   Is there such a one do you think, with us on the Zepher?

ACTOR TWO   No, there isn't. There would never be a movie about you and your deadbeat friends. It doesn't exist.

ACTOR ONE   How about something dramatic, a good story, but full of warm feeling?

EDNA   Maybe I should just go to bed. (*starting for her bedroom*)

43

ACTOR ONE A mystery. What about a mystery?

EDNA I don't know what I want.

ACTOR ONE There's got to be a good movie.

EDNA I just wish Andrew would come back. Where the heck is he?

ACTOR ONE (*bounding on top of the TV shelves, antenna raised high*) I have it! *Double Indemnity* on TCM in the original 1944 black and white. Remember how you loved that when it first came out? You'd only been married a few years. Barbara Stanwyck and Fred MacMurray, both in their prime, both top stars of their era, both fine actors, both beautiful, each in their unique way, especially her, and both—

EDNA Dead. They're both dead is what they are. Dead people. That's what you got for me. Fred MacMurray and Barbara Stanwyck. People I loved. John Wayne. Joan Crawford, Merle Oberon. I dreamed about those people. I had such a crush on Errol Flynn. You'll never know. Gary Cooper. My goodness. Edward G. Robinson. Oh he could be a devil. And that Jimmy Cagney. All of 'em. Dead. Every time I turn it on. Even The Three Stooges, and Abbott and Costello. They're gone too. Those sweet goofy guys. Who would want to harm them? Can you tell me that? It's not right. (*back at the table, the photo album*) Look at him. Do you see how beautiful he was? (*facing Actor One with the open album*) This is the man I married. But it's all gone. Everything. Everybody I ever liked or loved, and Andrew is walking around with my cane like a golf club. Off half the day practicing while I sit here. Do I want to go with him? Do I want to sit in the shop and watch him hitting and trying to learn?

Actor One sits at the table as Edna confides in her along with Actor Two who stands nearby.

No, I don't. I want him to sit here. I want him to look at me. To look right at me and talk to me. But off he goes. I want him to go. I want him to have fun. But then he calls. He ran into somebody else. They want to go out for dinner. Have a drink. Is that okay? What am I supposed to say? "No. Come home. The house, the house, the house is on fire." It's a cane not a golf club. I'd like to brain him with it. Wake him up to what's happening. I'm his mom and I'm dying. I'm goin' up in smoke and he's out there hitting balls into the sky. Not even playing. Just hitting. Trying to learn. Like it matters. Like there won't be time when I'm gone. I oughta break that cane over his head. That's what I oughta do. Break it over his head. Knock some sense into him. You see what I'm getting at.

ACTOR ONE Not exactly, but you should know, Edna, there is *The Golf Channel*, a whole channel devoted to golf. You could watch and learn.

EDNA I don't want to.

ACTOR ONE It shows big famous tournaments from different eras, and the announcers whisper, like it's all this big, important secret. You could watch it with Andrew, the two of you together.

EDNA Ohh, I'm gettin' so antsy.

ACTOR TWO It's a dark hole you're in Edna. Everything dissolving, fading, disappearing. You know it. I know it.

EDNA There's something between us, Andrew and me. I don't know what it is. It's not hitting golf balls. It's not him bein' out with his friends. I don't know what it is. But it's between us. Somethin' happened, and I don't know what or when. And I'm scared I'll never know. Why the heck don't he come home?

ACTOR TWO He's probably drinking, don't you think, carousing with his buddies.

EDNA Oh, now, don't start that and get me worryin' he's drunk and dead in the road.

Keys rattle in the door. She freezes, as Actor One scurries to the TV stand and Actor Two exits, as Andrew comes in.

ANDREW Hi, Mom.

EDNA   Hello, Andrew. Did you have a good time?

ANDREW   Yeah. How about you? What'd you do?

EDNA   Nothing much. Watched a little television.

ANDREW   Anything good?

EDNA   It was okay. Pretty good. I'm about ready for bed, though.

ANDREW   I hope I didn't stay out too late.

EDNA   I bet it did you good. Seein' your old friends.

ANDREW (*seeing the albums on the table*)   Were you looking at the photos?

EDNA   No. I was watchin' the boob tube and then something got me thinking about that last visit I had with Madeline. Pretty much the whole seventy years rolled into a couple miserable days. And the capper when I got home was this letter come from her accusing me of everything under the sun. And then she died.

ANDREW   I don't think you did anything wrong, Mom.

EDNA   It feels like I did. I shoulda let it go. I thought about phoning her a couple of times, but I never got around to it. I was afraid, I guess. That it'd just be more of the same. Anyway, I am really tuckered out. I better get under the covers before you have to carry me.

   She is on her way to her bedroom when he speaks.

ANDREW   You know, Mom, there's something I wanted to tell you. Something you said the other night got me thinking, and I talked to Sammy about it and he agreed. This was about Iowa City, and that you didn't get down there. I think we should do it now. If I arranged it would you go?

EDNA (*utterly surprised*)   Would I go down to Iowa city?

ANDREW   You and me. To see the specialists there.

EDNA You bet I would.

ANDREW Because we were at Sammy's cleaning up after golf and I called Dr. Grennel and told him what I was thinking and he thought it was a good idea.

EDNA He did? Dr. Grennel did?

ANDREW I said I'd see what you thought, but I was sure you'd be up for it, and that he should make the arrangements.

EDNA Is that right, Andrew? You did that today? You did that all today?

ANDREW Dr. Grennel said to give him a day or so to get it arranged. Send your files down there and then we could go.

EDNA But can you do that? Do we have time before you leave?

ANDREW He thought maybe Friday, and if not, I could stay on a couple extra of days.

EDNA But I mean, with your work and all, how can you?

ANDREW I think it's important we do this.

EDNA Ohh, that's so wonderful. I just can't believe it. This Friday?

ANDREW It's a day trip, you know.

EDNA Oh, but Andrew, Daddy's poor ole Buick is a junker. It'll never get us all that way down to Iowa City.

ANDREW I'll rent us a car. We can drive down in the morning, see them, and get back by bedtime easy. Or if they want us to stay over, we can.

EDNA They might see something everybody else missed.

ANDREW They're the best, right? Around here?

EDNA And even if they don't, we'll know we did all we could. It's been gnawin' at me. I can't believe it. I just can't. Thank you so much, Andrew. I'll call Jenny in the morning and tell her.

ANDREW   We'll have a little road trip, Mom. You and me.

EDNA   Jenny's gonna be so excited when she hears what we're doing. You kids are too good to me. Jenny says she feels so guilty sometimes about how far away she lives, but I say, no, that's your life. You have to live it. We raised you to be independent, I guess. Nobody ever thought you would be so far away, but we must have done something right— look how the both of you turned out. Never much money but always a lot of love.

She trembles saying this, at the edge of tears, and Andrew hugs and pats her.

ANDREW   That's for sure, Mom.

EDNA   I don't mean to put you kids through this. I really don't

ANDREW   It's okay. You're not. You're not doing anything, Mom. (*pause*) You better get some sleep, don't you think? I'm going to hit the hay, too. I'm whipped. It's been a long day. (*As they walk upstage together*)

EDNA   Long, but good. Couple minutes ago, I was ready to drop. Now I just hope I'm not too excited to sleep.

They part near her door; he moves toward his room.

ANDREW   'Night Mom. (*as he goes in*)

EDNA   'Night, Andrew. (*turning to enter her room, she stops*) By the way how'd you make out with those golf balls?

ANDREW   (*O.S.*)   Hit them pretty good.

EDNA   Good. See you in the morning.

She stands for a breath or two, then goes into her room.

BLACKOUT

Dark. TV sleeps on the floor. Andrew's door opens and he steps out in his underwear and T-shirt. He goes to the kitchen, where he grabs ice from the ice tray.

ACTOR ONE *(startled awake by the noise)*   What's going on?

ANDREW *(making his drink)*   Nothing. I'm restless.

ACTOR ONE *(getting her rabbit ears on)*   Wanna watch something?

ANDREW   Maybe in a minute.

ACTOR ONE   Okay. You'll be glad to know there's an abundance of highly distracting stuff available at this time of the night.

ANDREW   Maybe. *(crossing to sit in the recliner with his drink)*

ACTOR ONE   What else are you going to do?

ANDREW   I don't know.

ACTOR ONE   Are you just going to sit there and brood?

ANDREW   I'm thinking.

ACTOR ONE   About what?

ANDREW   I don't know, I said. I'm worried I stayed out too late. I think she's mad. I'm worried I upset her. I just got carried away and I can just feel it. She's in that little room mad, and she's right. I'm here to see her and I'm like—I'm—

Actor Two enters from near the kitchen.

ACTOR TWO   You're ungrateful and selfish.

ANDREW   I know. And my dad, too. I'm thinking about him. You know. She asks if I think about him lying out alone on that old dirt road and I don't. But I should. He lay out there for hours. Alone. His neck broken.

ACTOR ONE   Want to watch *Rescue Nine One One*?

ANDREW   What?

ACTOR ONE   *The Towering Inferno* is on TNT at 2 AM.

ACTOR TWO   Leave him alone. He has good reason to brood if he wants. Go ahead, if you feel it, Andrew. The dark miserable pull. Your mom is sad and she wants something. What does she think you can do? She's reaching out, and you feel it. Even though you're distant— you feel so distant—and yet she's reaching.

ANDREW   When I moved to the East I put thousands of miles of dirt and mountains between us—Illinois and Indiana, Ohio and Pennsylvania, and along with being real they were a measure of something else—of a need for a kind of protection, a barrier because of too much something—something dangerous to us both. She scared me somewhere along the line, and I scared her back, though we never spoke of this, or even admitted that it had happened.

ACTOR ONE   Are you just going to sit there and think like that? (*as Andrew takes a drink*) And drink.

ANDREW   But I have to get past it. I have to. Somehow. (*taking a big drink*)

ACTOR TWO   But you can't, can you. Why even try? Let it take you. It's who you are, isn't it. The sinking mood. The way you feel sometimes you'll never escape here, even though you've been gone for years, decades, you feel you can't ever get away. The way you feel you died here. Back in that other place, that little place. Those three little rooms. Long ago.

ACTOR ONE   But still—what good is brooding when you could be watching *Smokey and the Bandit*?

ANDREW (*rooting on the table*)   Where's the goddamn TV guide?

ACTOR ONE   It's there. Right where you're looking. *My Three Sons* is on right now. *Mary Tyler Moore*. Or there's some old movies—*Pat and Mike* with Spencer Tracy, or *Flaming Feather* with Sterling Hayden.

ANDREW   How about *The Three* goddamn *Stooges*. I'd like some *Abbott and Costello*. (*taking a big drink*)

ACTOR TWO   That's right. Have a drink. A big one. Don't you wish you still smoked? So you could take it deep. All that smoke. One of those I-don't-care-what-happens-to-me drags. Feel the hit. (*as he takes a drink*) That's right. There you go. Get trashed. It's your right. You died somewhere back here and you don't even know how or why.

ANDREW   I don't.

ACTOR TWO   What's that poem you love?

ANDREW   I don't love it any more.

ACTOR TWO   What is it, though? You know the one I mean. You read it in college. You loved it in—

ANDREW   I don't love it any more, I said.

ACTOR TWO   How does it go?

ANDREW   "After the first death there is no other."

ACTOR TWO   That's right.

ANDREW   Dylan Thomas.

ACTOR TWO   "After the first death there is no other."

ACTOR ONE   What does that even mean? It makes no sense.

ANDREW   It doesn't have to.

ACTOR TWO   It doesn't have to.

ANDREW   Anyway, it does. It makes a lot of sense. (*rushing to the kitchen table*) If you're me, anyway! I just can't believe she wants to get rid of her photo albums. I have to admit I'm shocked.

ACTOR TWO   It is shocking. And hurtful, too.

ANDREW (*at the albums on the table*)   There's me and Jenny in that little kitchen where we lived first. And Grandpa Donahue. He was a good guy. Now she wants to throw them out. "It hurts too much. It's too darn sad?" What is she talking about?

51

ACTOR TWO   It's very strange.

ANDREW   She's lived her life. She should want to sit and remember. Don't you think?

ACTOR ONE   She does! She just doesn't know how to tell you. On *Lifetime*—if you can stay up until three—there's a made-for-TV-movie from the seventies all about this man who is bitter about getting old but then his vivacious, bubbly granddaughter visits and he—

ANDREW   No, no. I'm asking why does she want to get rid of these? Doesn't she want to look back? Doesn't she know it's over? Her life? Isn't the pleasure for her to use the time left to relish the life she had?

ACTOR TWO   She's angry.

ANDREW   It seemed she was planning for this moment, planning to look back. She even put dates on the back—who was in them— where they were taken—so she could always remember. But— (*back to Actor Two*) What did you say?

ACTOR TWO   She's angry. She's bitter.

ANDREW   About what? Is she mad at me? Ohhh, you're nuts.

Thunder rumbles, as he moves to the tapes near the VCR.

I worked so hard on these tapes. I shot them for her and Dad. I had them in mind. I mean, I felt guilty being so far away—even though I had to be far away, but—but— So I shot these tapes and I copied them. I had a machine to copy them and then . . .

He hands a tape to Actor One, who fits it into the VCR under her.

. . . I'd pack them up and mail them out, and I'd get these excited phone calls from Mom and Dad. From both of them. Look at how many and now, she—she—

ACTOR ONE   Ohh, look, Andrew. It's you. And your kids. Oh, and so many happy, bubbly people. It's a party.

Andrew stares. More thunder, as rain starts. Actor Two sits in Edna's recliner to watch.

ANDREW   A birthday party. One of the kids is having a birthday—

ACTOR ONE   Which one? Oh, I love bringing all this to you—beaming with all this light and wonder—the lawn so gleaming and green and—

ANDREW   It's Angela's birthday party. And there's Nick. Little Nick.

ACTOR ONE   See his big cowboy hat—his too big cowboy hat—so big it keeps falling over his eyes. Oh, Andrew, you look so happy.

ANDREW   They're so little. Look how little they are.

ACTOR TWO   So much of your life is over.

ANDREW   What?

ACTOR TWO   So much of your life is over, Andrew,

EDNA   Andrew? Andrew is that you? *(entering in her robe)* What are you doing up? Goodness, what time is it?

ANDREW   Did I wake you? Sorry.

Actor Two eases upstage.

EDNA   It was the thunder, I think. What's that you're watching? *(then she sees)* Ohh, yeah, cute. Would you look at that Nicky, the poor child. His hat don't fit.

ANDREW   It was mine. He wanted to wear it.

EDNA   It's one of the birthday parties. There's the big cake. Always a big cake. *(sitting in the recliner)*

ANDREW   Angela's seventh, I think.

Thunder, and she looks off.

EDNA   Darn stuff woke me up out of a sound sleep, then I heard voices out here and I thought, "where am I?"

ANDREW   Where am I, who am I, what am I?

EDNA   Something like that. Oh, look at that Angela dancing now. A regular little ballerina.

ACTOR ONE   Here comes a clown. So many excited children. Look at them all. And a pony. A fortune teller, even. Pony rides. Balloons. And bright sun everywhere.

EDNA   Daddy loved lookin' at little Nicky with that hat fallin' down over his eyes, let me tell you. Laughed himself silly.

ANDREW   Did he?

EDNA   Tears commin' out of his eyes. Once you called and told us how to get it to back up, we'd watch it again and again.

ANDREW   Then why get rid of them?

EDNA   Let's not start that again.

ACTOR ONE   Watch! She's going to blow out the candles. One, two, three—

Booming thunder makes them wince.

ANDREW   Whoa, that sounded close.

EDNA   Right on top of us. Ohh, Andrew, I hope this rain doesn't mess up our trip.

ANDREW   We'll just drive in the rain, if we have to, Mom. If it's pouring we'll just take our time.

EDNA   We get some crazy weather out here. Tornadoes even, you know that.

Thunder, distant but ominous, as they look up.

ANDREW   Scawwwy.

EDNA   Vewwwy scawwweey.

Fading lights, distant thunder.

END OF ACT ONE

ACT TWO

Edna's apartment. Empty. The telephone rings: one, two, three, four times, and then there is the clatter of keys as the front door opens and Edna, battling to get in before the ringing stops, runs to the phone and grabs it up.

EDNA Hello. Hello. Oh, Jenny hi. Hi. Goodness. We just got back. Just this second. The phone was ringing; I was in the hall. I was thinking it might be one of the doctors. So I just about busted a gut getting in here. Got so flustered I couldn't get my key in right. No, no, I'm not disappointed it's you. Goodness no. Let me catch my breath. He's outside. Parking the car. The courtyard lot was pretty jammed. Andrew was unloading and I was waiting, but then I heard the phone. Somebody's having a party of some kind, it looks like. No, I don't know who. There's some young people moved into building D, the one on the corner. What? Uh uh, no, the other corner. *(as she sits a sense of the trip as miraculous comes over her, all omens good)* What a trip we had. It was a regular adventure. That's what it was. The things that happened. You know all that rain we were having, it just went away. It just went away. The weather was perfect. It was like we were meant to go. Oh, boy. He was a gem, this Dr. Spencer. Really took his time with me. Asked me all these questions and I could see how he thought about my answers like it really mattered what I said.

Andrew comes in loaded down with their overnight bags, his computer bag, trash from the car.

Oooop, here's Andrew.

ANDREW Who's that?

EDNA Jenny. The phone was ringing when I got to the door. I just made it.

ANDREW   Hi, Jenny.

Though he unpacks, Andrew hovers, tracking Edna's report on the trip.

EDNA (*into the phone*)   Andrew says hi. What? Oh, sure I know that.

ANDREW   What?

EDNA (*to Andrew*)   That she would have called back. (*into phone*) Of course you would have. (*to Andrew*) She was dying to know how it all went.

ANDREW (*an important, almost mystical detail*)   Did you tell her about the flat tire?

EDNA (*into phone*)   You'll never guess, Jenny, but we had a flat tire. Yes we did. What? No, it wasn't dangerous. It got us there fine, but when we came back after talking to the doctors, the darn thing was flat as a pancake. No, no, he didn't have to fix it. He didn't bother. He just got us a new car. (*to Andrew*) Isn't that right, Andrew.

ANDREW (*another almost mystical detail*)   And we got lost.

EDNA (*into phone*)   We got lost, too. Yes. I don't know exactly, but not for long. (*to Andrew*) How long were we off course would you say?

ANDREW   Maybe twenty minutes out of our way. Not bad.

EDNA (*into phone*)   He says we went about twenty minutes out of our way. But it was fun. Yes, it was, if you want to know the truth. We laughed ourselves silly. Had a good time in our own crazy way. (*to Andrew*) Didn't we Andrew?

ANDREW   Yes we did. Couple of fools on the road.

EDNA (*into phone*)   That part of the state gets real flat, if you remember. Nothing but flat. We wandered off down this road and all of a sudden Andrew says, "I think we're lost." And we were.

She speaks with increasing awe, while Andrew listens and gets glasses of water for them both.

The two of us out in the middle of nowhere—I mean fields all around. Some of it was corn the way it is this time of year, and there were cows way off. And we take it for granted. But being lost, I looked at it. The sun was down but not gone. The whole thing was picturesque, all of a sudden. It was, wasn't it, Andrew.

ANDREW Yes, it was. We got lost because we changed cars.

EDNA What's that?

ANDREW We got lost because we changed cars.

EDNA (*into phone*) He says we got lost because we changed cars. I don't know. (*to Andrew*) She says to ask you how that would work?

ANDREW The directions from the rental company were in the old car. The first car. The one with the flat tire, and I forgot to take them with me when we moved to the new one.

EDNA Is that what happened? I never knew. (*into the phone*) What Jenny? I don't think we know. (*to Andrew*) We don't know what made the tire go flat, do we?

ANDREW Not really. Slow leak of some kind. (*moving to settle in his recliner*)

EDNA (*into phone*) Slow leak, he thinks. Yes. Well, we come back after the doctor and we don't get to drive a foot before there's a terrible noise. He gets out and says, "Flat tire, Mom." Now we're stuck, I think, but he says not to worry. Off he goes back into all these doctor's offices to find a pay phone. And the place is huge, let me tell you. I gotta sit tight. Next thing I know I see him walking back and before he can even tell me, this other car is pulling up. They deliver it right to us. This young kid. And it's better than the first one, if you ask me? (*to Andrew*) Wouldn't you say so, Andrew?

ANDREW As good or better.

EDNA (*into phone*) And the kid that brought it is real pleasant. He came with all the paperwork ready. Andrew only has to sign a couple times and off we go. And if the poor kid apologized once, he apologized ten times for any inconvenience, like it's his fault the tire went flat. Now that's a good company.

ANDREW   Enterprise.

EDNA (*to Andrew*)   What's that?

ANDREW   That's the name of the company.

EDNA   Oh, sure. They have a great reputation here in town. (*into phone*) Enterprise. That's the company, Jenny. Take my advice and write that down if you ever need to rent a car at some point in the future. (*beat*) Okay. (*to Andrew*) She wants to talk to you.

ANDREW   Sure. (*moving to her, hovering to take the phone*)

EDNA   Bye, Honey. Thanks for calling. (*beat*) Yes, we will. You bet. We get any news, you will hear from us. Day or night.

She hands the phone to Andrew, and moves off to the armchair to sit, remove her shoes, rub her feet one on the other.

ANDREW (*into phone*)   Hi. Yeah. It was a good time. The doctor was very good, I thought. Serious, thoughtful.

EDNA   He had an aura about him.

ANDREW   Mom says he had an aura about him.

EDNA   You knew after a couple seconds—you could just tell—this one knows his business.

ANDREW (*to Edna*)   That's for sure, Mom. (*into phone*) You could see why he was situated the way he was at Iowa City. It was kind of amazing.

EDNA   Whata you mean?

ANDREW   What?

EDNA   What was amazing?

ANDREW   How much time he spent. How thoroughly he'd gone over your file, X-rays and—well, all of it.

EDNA   Why's that amazing?

ANDREW   I don't know. I don't know if I expected that.

EDNA   Let me talk to her. (*reaching for the phone without moving from the chair as Andrew hurries to give the phone to her*) We sat right in front of his desk. Two nice comfortable chairs. Big wide armrests. Big desk, too. Pictures of his family, and all those certificates on the wall. Awards, too. Solid, you felt, and he leaned there, looking right at you. He didn't make any crazy promises, but he wanted a couple X-rays of his own, and some blood work. I could just feel it. He was gonna look between the cracks, you know. Move the furniture if he had to. He wasn't going to settle for what Grennel and his gang down here at the HMO might think—where they don't even know to give a person a Pap smear and a pelvic exam. I know, it's water over the damn. But this Dr. Spencer, I tell you, he had a voice on him— soothing as all get out. And this quality—this quality about him like a detective. Anyway, here's Andrew.

She holds the phone out for Andrew, who takes it, and then paces away into the kitchen.

ANDREW (*into phone*)   Hi. Yeah. So that's what we know so far. No, no, I'm really glad we went. Flat tire and all. Getting lost. Actually, like Mom says, that was fun. I don't know. We were just lost, you know and it was like—we weren't quite ourselves (*to Edna*) Does that make sense, Mom?

EDNA   I'd say so. We were just these two driving around.

ANDREW (*into the phone, as he sits down at the kitchen table*)   We were about halfway back, and there was a turn—I'd left the directions, so I didn't know it was coming up, so I wasn't looking for it. (*pause*) You could be right. I don't know. I guess maybe I am being a little guarded about the visit. I don't mean to be . . . Mom saw it the way she says, and it's all true. All she says is true. I'm just trying to keep my expectations from getting too unrealistic, and hers too, so we don't get too optimistic.

EDNA   See that's where we disagree. Why not be optimistic? There's nothing unreal about a little optimism.

Edna moves to the kitchen table, where she leans over the vase and flowers still there.

ANDREW   Well, sure. No, no, Jenny. You're right. You're both right. Why not go with it?

EDNA (*examining the flowers*)   That's just the feeling I had. That's how it all seemed to me. You know what, Andrew? I was thinking the time had come to throw these flowers out, but they still smell kinda nice don't you think? Or do you disagree? (*sticking the flowers under his nose*)

ANDREW (*sniffing the flowers*)   No, no.

EDNA (*moving to the sink where she gets water in a glass*)   And they're pretty in their own way. I'm gonna change the water.

ANDREW (*into phone*)   What, Jenny? Can you hold on? Mom's trying to tell me something. (*to Edna*) What was that, Mom?

EDNA   It's nothing. You finish talking to Jenny.

ANDREW   But what'd you say?

EDNA (*mixing sugar into the water*)   I'm gonna put some sugar in the water. Mindy says—or maybe it was Bernice—I think it was Bernice—oh, no, what the heck, it was Donna—that if you put a little sugar in the water, it helps flowers along. Gives 'em a little pep. So I'll try that. What do you think?

ANDREW   Sure.

EDNA   They're doin' their best. And that's good enough. Why not help 'em out—give 'em a fighting chance? I gotta change these shoes.

ANDREW   What's that, Mom? Hold on, Jenny.

EDNA (*talking to the flowers and pouring the sugar water to the vase*)   Gonna give you a little sugar water. So I guess you got a little sweet tooth. (*moving toward her room*) I wore these shoes to make a nice impression on Dr. Spencer, but they pinch like the dickens.

He watches her go into her room.

ANDREW (*into the phone*) She's going to change her shoes. And she's talking to the flowers.

beat

Do I? I don't feel sarcastic. So I don't see how I could sound that way. I mean, I—there's just a lot— But I will tell you this. I am glad we went. If only for the trip. That funny little—I don't know—interlude? But do you know what, I think I should call you back. Maybe after she's in bed. No, she's good over all. Half the time you'd never know she was sick. Her spirits? Her spirits are good. I should tell you though, she says she sees Dad sometimes. No. In the apartment. Shuffling around with his walker. No. I haven't. Not hide nor hair, but a friend of mine, his wife died and the palliative care doctor told him not to be surprised if he saw her sitting at the foot of his bed. That's right. Yes, after she was dead. Yes, yes. The palliative care doctor. So I guess it's maybe common. Listen. I've been driving and parking, sitting with doctors since sunup. So I need to—something. Okay. Talk soon. Sorry if I'm grumpy or defensive or sarcastic or whatever I am. Bye.

Pacing now near the recliner, he hangs up and sits. Edna comes out in her nightgown, robe, and house slippers.

EDNA I ended up changin' more than my shoes.

ANDREW Time to get comfortable.

EDNA Should I try and rustle up a little something for us to eat?

ANDREW I'm stuffed, Mom.

EDNA That burger filled me up, I know that. But you! (*as she sits in her recliner*) I never saw anybody eat so much yogurt in my life. And plain, too.

ANDREW I had a salad.

EDNA You know what? I got to admit it. I'm bushed. I think I'm going to hit the hay. If I can manage to stand back up. Jenny sounded excited though, didn't she?

ANDREW We had a big day. I'm kinda wiped out myself.

EDNA I bet you are. All that drivin' and maps and all. I walked into the bedroom full of pep, and all of a sudden I just about fell over. I better check my blood sugar. (*picking up the gauge she looks at it, then stands*) Can I get you anything before I go?

ANDREW I'm fine, Mom.

EDNA I think I'm just tired. Things feel different when my sugar is bad. (*pausing on her way to her room*) I wanna thank you for today, Andrew.

ANDREW C'mon, Mom. You don't have to.

EDNA I know I don't have to. But I'm gonna remember this day. This was one of the best days ever.

ANDREW It was.

EDNA The two of us alone. That's what made it so special. "I think we're lost, Mom." "We got a flat tire, Mom." Me sittin' and waitin' for you to come back. All these little moments. They keep goin' through my head, you know.

ANDREW I know what you mean.

EDNA Do you? Good. (*after a few step toward her room, she stops*) See you in the morning. I love sayin' it.

ANDREW See you in the morning.

He watches her go, and then turns toward the TV area as Actor One bounds on with a satellite dish held high over her head.

ACTOR ONE Hi. (*as he gazes at her, and leans back in the recliner*) Hi, hi, hi.

ANDREW I really need to zone out.

ACTOR ONE Me, too. I've been waiting.

ANDREW Any movies?

Aiming the remote, he turns the TV on.

ACTOR ONE Of course. How about . . . (*dramatic music and she aims the dish high*) . . . *Hell in the Pacific* with Lee Marvin.

ANDREW Maybe. Maybe.

ACTOR ONE What's your preference? Or *The Sandpiper*. (*different music*) *The Sandpiper* with Elizabeth Taylor.

ANDREW No.

ACTOR ONE (*different music; another angle for the dish*)   *Breaker Morant?*

ANDREW What was that first one?

ACTOR ONE Maybe something funny?

ANDREW I think I'll just hop.

ACTOR ONE Okay. Sure. (*hastening to the TV stand as Andrew changes the channel*) In only a week, skin starts becoming firmer and more radiant. Clinically proven to reduce the appearance of—(*Andrew changes the channel*) He did! I swear it! He picked up the hammer and the book.

As the lights go black.

Scene II

Edna sleeps. Actor Two sits toward the bottom of her bed. She bolts up facing Actor Two.

EDNA Oh, we had such a wonderful trip, me and Andrew. Don't take away the special way I'm feeling.

ACTOR TWO Of course not. Never.

EDNA Don't take it away.

ACTOR TWO Of course not. Never. But don't you think it makes everything worse, somehow having a time like that? Why wasn't it always that way? Why wasn't it that way always?

EDNA I don't know. I'm just trying to be happy with what I got.

ACTOR TWO But why did you have to be lost in the middle of nowhere to feel so close? Why did you have to be lost in the middle of nowhere? So much mystery in your simple life. So much you don't understand. Why did you have to be lost in the middle of nowhere?

EDNA You're doin' something to me. I'm feeling kind of funny—different, like you're doin' something deep and dark and secret and no good.

ACTOR TWO I'm not. No, no. But what if you die with the trouble between you and Andrew unsettled? Because it's going to happen. You've seen others. So many others. And it'll be your time soon. And you're scared. It's scary.

EDNA What do you want?

ACTOR TWO (*he faces her*) To live. With you, my one and only. If only you'd stop fighting. I get tired, too, Edna. I exist against all odds. Generations spawned; alliances forged within the mutant horde I lead to survive in the harshest landscape. I must have you.

EDNA You're like an animal. A savage wild animal.

ACTOR TWO (*incensed*) Even though you assault me with your T cells with their terrible claws; and NK cells. Madmen, some of them—determined to butcher me if I don't fly the proper flag. And so I raise false flags. I elude them. My ingenuity, my cunning beyond anything they—

EDNA Get away from me. Get away. (*he stays where he is*) Can't you hear me? I'm telling you to get away and stay away. (*he doesn't move*) I don't know what you're doing.

ACTOR TWO I am too powerful. Give up. You need to rest.

She turns away, flopping down.

EDNA I do. I really want to.

ACTOR TWO Good. (*as she begins to relax*) Edna. Edna.

EDNA What?

ACTOR TWO I think you should admit that you're lying about Doctor Spencer.

EDNA I am not.

ACTOR TWO You know you are. All that confidence and hope. You don't really believe he's going to come up with something special that nobody else ever thought of and then give it to you. Why would he go to all that trouble for the likes of you? You don't matter. He doesn't care. No one cares. Not even Andrew.

EDNA He does too.

ACTOR TWO Not in the way you'd like. You know what he thinks. What they all think. That you're old, and you're done with your life. That you've lived it and you knew what you were doing and so you got everything you wanted out of it. Like it doesn't cling to you.

Edna sits up, so they face each other on her bed.

EDNA But it does. All the things you live, they cling to you. Half the time you're so confused you don't know what you're doing. You do things, and you try, and you know you're getting older, but what the heck? So is everybody else. And then you're old. All of a sudden.

ACTOR TWO And it's like you didn't see it coming. You should have. But you didn't.

EDNA Ohh, boy. Oh darn.

ACTOR TWO What?

EDNA I don't know if I took my Lasix pill. I can't remember. I should take it if I didn't.

ACTOR TWO   It doesn't matter.

EDNA   But I don't know if I took my Lasix pill.

ACTOR TWO   Listen to me. It doesn't matter.

EDNA   I can't remember, I'm tellin' you. I'm gonna pray. (*putting on a little light, picking up her glasses*) Maybe that'll calm me down a little.

ACTOR TWO   It's pointless, you know.

EDNA   Well, we'll just see about that. There's angels, you know, and Saint Peregrine might just send one to help me.

ACTOR TWO   What's an angel?

Disgusted with him, she starts to read her prayer. Actor Two paces around her bed, along the front, along the back. Again the front.

EDNA   O great Saint Perigrine, you who have been called The Mighty, "The Wonder-Worker" because of the numerous miracles which you have obtained from God for those who have had recourse to you—you who for so many years bore in your own flesh this cancerous disease that destroys the very fiber of our being—you who had recourse to the source of all grace when the power of man could do no more—you who were favored with the vision of Jesus coming down from His Cross to heal your affliction—ask of God and Our Lady for the cure of these sick persons who we entrust to you. So please pray for . . . me. For Edna. And help Doctor Spencer figure out something to help me. And . . . please help me remember if I took my Lasix pill. (*as he sits at the foot of the bed*) Aided in this way by your powerful intercession, we shall sing to God now and— (*her eyes open*) I did. I took it. I took my pill.

ACTOR TWO   Are you sure?

EDNA   When I first came in here. I just remembered. (*lying back down slowly*) And . . . we shall sing to God now and for all eternity a song of gratitude for His great goodness and mercy. Amen.

ACTOR TWO   I don't think you took your pill, Edna.

EDNA   I did, too. (*sinking back*) I took it.

ACTOR TWO   All right. Of course. But you know you're not sure.
Edna. (*realizing she sleeps*) Edna? And so ends the little life of another
day. Do you see how easy it is to give up? Hiding in sleep, are you?
Hiding in dreams. I'll follow you there. Do you see me? Is that me?
Yes, it is. I'm there with you. I've got you!

Edna stirs, sits up, looking around as he slips out the door. Lights go black.

SCENE III

Lights up on Andrew in the recliner with Actor One on his lap.

ANDREW   My Dad drove his car into a tree when he was seventy
years old and he broke his neck. He was a lover of Edgar Allen Poe
stories—you know those creepy doomed people—and after the car
crashed—it was on a back road—a dirt road, and after it crashed,
he couldn't move because he was paralyzed and it was dark. It was
dark and no one came for hours. He was terrified that the car would
burst into flame, or he would die from the injury. He was alone and
he screamed and cried, he told me. He begged, but no one came. Of
course someone did come. A passerby. But when he told it, he was
there alone and no one came.

ACTOR ONE   Wanna watch *Bay Watch*?

ANDREW   No.

ACTOR ONE   Lots of titties. Nipples showing through the spandex.

ANDREW   I know.

ACTOR ONE   Take a look.

ANDREW   I know. But I feel—I feel like I'm in the middle of a
ghost story.

ACTOR ONE   Wanna watch one? *Twilight Zone—Tales of the Crypt—
The Night Stalker—Dark Shadows?*

ANDREW   I want to know what Dad was thinking, trapped like that. Like in that Edgar Allan Poe story, where this man buries alive this other man behind a wall. Brick by brick. And they talk, as it's happening. The guy getting buried tries to be tough and brave at first—he jokes that he's being buried alive. But in the end he begs. I wonder if laying out there in the dark unable to move, Dad thought about that story.

ACTOR ONE   No. No. He thought about you. How he loved you. How he wanted to live to see you again. He got his strength from thinking about you.

ANDREW   I have to say I really have my doubts about that.

ACTOR ONE   On *Rescue Nine One One*, we had this one—check the guide—it might be on again.

ANDREW   He loved rescue stories.

ACTOR ONE   Who? Your Dad? Well, this was a really thrilling one, even though it started off much worse than what happened to your dad, because this car went into a lake and the driver was knocked unconscious, but then an expert swimmer happened by and saved both the man and the dog.

ANDREW   There was a dog involved?

ACTOR ONE   Yes. Buster was his name. And the expert swimmer saved him, too. And afterwards the man said he'd fought to live so he could see his family again.

ANDREW   Dad would have loved that one. Actually, he told rescue stories. About his own life. His friends always did the right thing— they won every fight, they beat up every bully. If somebody insulted them, they hauled off and smacked them in the mouth. Or if some crook or a kind of con man tried to take advantage of them, they suddenly knew how to outsmart the guy. There was no last of the ninth where one of them didn't hit a home run. Nobody ever struck out.

ACTOR ONE   They sound like pretty wonderful stories.

ANDREW   But they're bullshit. Don't you see? Edgar Allan Poe and rescue stories? That makes no sense. Because in Edgar Allan Poe stories nobody ever gets rescued. Not ever.

ACTOR ONE   *Rescue Nine One One* had this other thrilling, inspiring episode where this house started to burn and the teenage son, who was out past curfew, came home just in time to save everybody.

ANDREW   You know what? You're just stupid.

ACTOR ONE   Go to channel 29. (*Andrew looks at her, doubtfully*) Go on. Then you'll see. I mean it. Go! (*hurrying to the TV stand*) It's a made-for-TV movie called *So Little Time*, and the dad is sick and the son, Gary, has been angry for years but right here, right now—look, I'm telling you—hurry—

Andrew turns on the TV and music comes on.

—his dad is telling Gary he loves him. And these words are raising up this lost, lost feeling in Gary, so he's hugging his dad and weeping and his tears are beautiful and pure because of what his dad is telling him on his deathbed and the music is soaring and sad, but triumphant.

ANDREW   That's ridiculous.

ACTOR ONE   It is not.

ANDREW   You're an asshole. (*pacing to the kitchen for a drink*)

ACTOR ONE   You're an asshole. Not loving your father.

ANDREW   I loved him.

ACTOR ONE   Just because you don't have those kinds of feelings, Andrew, doesn't mean other people don't, because they do.

ANDREW   His stories were bullshit. Like yours! It wasn't the truth. I never got to know him. And I never would have, not even if he lived to be a hundred. His goddamn stories kept me from getting to know him.

70

ACTOR ONE (*annoyed*) Maybe you should watch something more compatible with your nasty, negative, unpleasant mood. On *Life Stories* "a drug dealer becomes a quadriplegic."

ANDREW What?

ACTOR ONE You tell me. *Scooby Doo!* (*hurrying to him*) Or *Baseball Tonight* in rerun. *Mad About You* starts in eight minutes.

ANDREW No, no, no. (*throwing ice in a glass, he pours a drink*)

ACTOR ONE Paul looses his shoes while running after a bus because Jamie drove away without him.

ANDREW There was something in the way, I'm telling you. Something keeping Dad from me—his goddamn stories, or something—I couldn't get at. I never did get at it.

ACTOR ONE You're kind of angry. Maybe there's a fight on. I bet you'd like to see a fight.

ANDREW What one?

ACTOR ONE Basilio and Robinson. Channel 26.

As Actor Two steps in behind the recliners. He wears a sweater belonging to Andrew's father.

ACTOR TWO What was terrible, Andrew?

ANDREW (*to Actor Two*) I wanted to hear him; I wanted to hear him, but I couldn't. He was ill and old and trying to talk to me—telling those same damn stories—and I think he thought he was telling me about himself, but it was just those stories and I couldn't listen. I would go off into a haze. And then I would ask him a question and he would go off into a haze. It made me disgusted with myself that I did that.

ACTOR ONE Basilio and Robinson. Basilio and Robinson. C'mon. You can watch Robinson beat the crap out of Basilio.

ANDREW (*turning to Actor One, his back to Actor Two*) Maybe. It was terrible because he was in his chair and I was in the other and time was running out. We were right next to each other in terms of where we were sitting, but I was miles from him—or years—and he was just as far from me. And then one day, when he was dead, I thought to myself—or the thought came to me —

Actor Two sits in his recliner, and Andrew turns to face him.

I hated your rescue stories Dad, and do you know why? Because I didn't believe them, and do you know why? Because nobody ever rescued me from you. That's why. But then thinking that just made everything worse.

ACTOR ONE Maybe boxing's not such a good idea.

ANDREW No. It's a great idea. Channel 26? Basilio and Robinson!

Actor Two hurries to the TV stand.

It'll be the way it was, right Dad? We'd sit in these chairs and watch the fighters go at it.

Faint cheers and crowd noise.

ACTOR ONE Basilio is battered, his left eye swollen shut. Robinson's left is straight as a bullet out from his shoulder. Basilio is half blind.

ACTOR TWO He's half blind. He bobs and weaves.

ANDREW He bobs and weaves, but there's nowhere to go. Nowhere to hide to get away from you. Out of control. Crazy out of your mind—chasing me with that goddamn belt.

ACTOR ONE Basilio lands a wild right, and Robinson retaliates with a brutal left hook, a storm of lefts, a booming upper cut, a long thundering right.

ANDREW (*to Actor Two*) You were just frustrated and disappointed and sad because so many things went wrong for you. (*staring at Actor Two, who never looks at Andrew*) Isn't that right, Dad. Almost everything. Maybe that's why you loved Poe—maybe you loved those doomed frightened people, those terrified, pitiful figures, because that's how you felt. And you loved rescue stories, simple heroics because you wanted someone to rescue you.

ACTOR ONE   Basilio is bent down like he's bowing to Robinson who hammers lefts and rights into Basilio's ribs.

ANDREW (*to Actor Two*)   You would sit gazing off, and I would stare at you wondering, What were you thinking? What were you really thinking? Were you trying to figure out some way to rescue yourself? Or maybe you hoped I'd rescue you. But I couldn't. You knocked me around once too often.

ACTOR ONE   Basilio straightens and Robinson's left finds him, like a dagger turning his eye into raw bloody hamburger.

ACTOR TWO   Nobody's going to rescue Basilio.

ACTOR ONE   Nobody's going to rescue Basilio.

ANDREW   No. Nobody's going to rescue Basilio.

Fading lights to BLACKOUT

SCENE IV

Evening light. The phone rings: one, two, three.

EDNA (*O.S.*)   Andrew? Andrew? Answer the darn phone!

As toilet flushes, Edna rushes from the bathroom to the phone, looking around as she goes.

EDNA   Hang on. I'm commin'. (*grabbing up the phone*) Hello. What? No, there is no such person at this number. No, he won't be back. You have a wrong number. That's right. Okay. No bother.

She hangs up, and turns back into the kitchen, looking around for Andrew as the phone rings. She hurries back.

EDNA   Hello. Oh, Dr. Spencer. Hello. (*she listens*) I see. Uh huh. (*she listens*) Uh huh. So that's the deal then. Well, it didn't hurt to try. I have to admit it I had my hopes up a little. Oh, just about to have some coffee. No, he's not here just this second. But I know he enjoyed talking to you, too. He's leaving tomorrow. Lives out East. Family and all there. So he's got to go. But I'll tell him. And I want to tell you I appreciate you taking the time to try.

   beat

Yes. Okay, then. And I appreciate the way you and your helpers treated us. First-class. And you should know, we had a great trip down there, my son and me. The two of us. That ride through all those beautiful fields. That's right. That's what counts. Okay then.

   beat

Bye. (*hanging up, moving toward the sink*) Shoot. Darn it anyhow.

   The phone rings, and she answers, as Andrew comes in the front door carrying an arm load of laundry.

Hello. Didn't we just speak? This Wilbur person you're after is not here. No, I don't think he will be back later—at least I sure hope not. He doesn't live here. (*growing infuriated, she pauses and then erupts*) No, darn you. What in the heck is wrong with you? Now just stop calling. (*slamming the phone down*)

ANDREW   What was all that?

EDNA   I thought you were out here and by the time I figured out you'd gone off, it was five or six rings. I came close to breaking my neck getting here.

   Andrew has placed a suitcase near the recliner where he's piled the clothes he carried in.

ANDREW   I went down to the basement to get my laundry out of the dryer. I thought I'd get organized, do a little packing.

EDNA   Oh.

Edna watches closely, as Andrew folds the clothing, tucks socks into each other, gathering it all on the recliner.

ANDREW I guess we're not going to get to that movie we talked about.

EDNA Nope. No, no. The time just goes. Looks like there's a lot when you lookin' forward to it. Oh my goodness, you're thinkin', so many days and nights. It seems an eternity, but then it's gone faster than anybody woulda ever thought.

ANDREW At least we got a few things done.

EDNA Oh, yeah. Got to Iowa City.

ANDREW Solved the mystery of your check book.

EDNA It was a good visit. I know you gotta go—you got your life and all—so many things to take care of I don't know how you keep track of it all with your work and the kids. Flyin' here and there. Makes me dizzy just thinkin' about it.

ANDREW Makes me dizzy, too, Mom. Sometimes.

EDNA I would think so. And them dogs. They gotta take up time too, and money with the vets and all. And food. Four dogs. That's gotta cost a pretty penny. And it all falls to you, I bet, takin' care of them.

ANDREW A lot of it.

EDNA Sure. But you always loved dogs. From the time you first saw one, but we couldn't have a dog in that poor little apartment, and even when we got the house, it wasn't big enough and no yard, the way it was laid out right up against that bluff. (*with everything packed Andrew zippers the suitcase shut, and she winces*) You know what I hate? Oh, I just hate it. The sound of them zippers. It just cuts through me. I could start bawlin'. Sharp as a knife.

ANDREW The zippers?

EDNA Sure. Don't you see? Visits over. That's what it tells me. Gonna be alone, soon. You or Jenny packing up to go—zip zip. I just hate it.

ANDREW   I gotta pack.

EDNA   Andrew. Sure. But you got all morning tomorrow. I don't see why you have to do it now.

ANDREW   I can stop.

Andrew heads with everything toward his room.

EDNA   Because what it feels like is you just can't wait to get out of here as fast and as far away as possible.

ANDREW   No, no. I wish I could stay longer. I just didn't want to leave it all to the last minute. I was just trying to get a head start.

EDNA   You know best, and I don't want you to forget anything.

ANDREW (*exiting his room*)   You know it's not that late—we could actually make it to that movie, if you wanted.

EDNA   What time is it?

The cuckoo clock goes off seven times, the little bird going in and out.

Oh, now isn't that the darndest thing. I thought you fixed him so he wouldn't do that.

ANDREW   I missed it. I started him up again just a bit ago.

EDNA   Oh, sure. You're gettin ready to leave. Why not turn him on? Can't bother you once you're gone.

Wounded Andrew starts for the bathroom, but falters, as she gazes at the clock. He doesn't know what to do with himself.

Reminds me of my dad, you know. Hand carved. Would you look at that bird—so real looking. Ready to fly. And the leaves with veins in 'em even. He was a handy one, my dad.

ANDREW   Yes, he was.

EDNA   I can see it like it was yesterday—the first time he brought it up from the basement where he built it.

Andrew spies the newspaper on the kitchen table. He takes refuge, standing, reading, looking down. Edna fixes on him more and more, almost accusatory.

Proud as a peacock. Set it up, and showed how the weights worked, and what made the cuckoo go in and out. I was a kid. A teenager. Lord, lord. Cuckoo. It was quite a thing back then. And him makin' it by hand. You know what I mean.

ANDREW (*sticking with the paper*)   Yes, I do.

EDNA   Kids today wouldn't think twice about it, all the gadgets they got. But little Nicky liked it.

ANDREW   Yes, he did.

EDNA   First time. "What's it doin' Grandma?" "Tellin' us what time it is, Honey," I told him. "But how does it know what time it is?" Cute! Let me tell you, cute as a button. He'd stand lookin' up like he was waitin' to catch it.

ANDREW (*glancing at her, but still with the paper*)   I remember.

EDNA   I'd like Nicky to have that clock when I'm gone. I'd like to leave it to him.

ANDREW (*surprised*)   Oh, sure. That'd be nice. (*moving to the refrigerator for a glass of water*)

EDNA   Can you see to that for me, Andrew?

ANDREW   Sure.

EDNA   I have to say it, Andrew. I worry sometimes you don't have that special feeling. That family feeling.

ANDREW (*flaring with anger*)   I hear you, Mom. You'd like me to see that Nicky gets the clock. Got it.

He sits at the table, grabbing up the newspaper, as she stalks to her recliner and takes up her crocheting.

EDNA   And let me tell you another thing, I'll be glad you got him workin' again once you're gone. I like it when I'm here alone, and out he comes with his little cuckoo. Kind of keeps me company. Him and me.

They sit in silence, Andrew at the table, Edna in the recliner. Until he puts down the paper and looks at her.

ANDREW   You remember the Whitfield Hotel fire?

EDNA   You mean the one we had here in town? Oh. Sure. Terrible thing. Those poor people. Is there something in the paper?

ANDREW   Well— (*beat*) No.

EDNA   You're not gonna try and tell me you remember it. That don't seem possible.

ANDREW   I think I do. How'd it happen?

EDNA   The fire? Darned if I know.

ANDREW   No, I mean, how'd it happen that I ended up there?

EDNA   Oh I hope you're not gonna blame me for somethin' way back that I done when people didn't know any better. I don't know what we were thinkin', takin' you down there. Times were different. People were different back then. They just did things, you know. There weren't all these people like Dr. Laura on the radio tellin' you how to take care of kids. People were so riled up about that fire. Everybody was phonin' everybody and headin down there to see for themselves. I don't know who phoned us, but Daddy wanted to go. Real bad. You know him. It was history in the making. Terrible, just terrible. You were in bed I'm sure. What were you, five or six?

ANDREW   Six. It was 1946.

EDNA   You're not sayin' you remember the date.

ANDREW   No, I got this down at the library. The other day. (*taking a Xerox of an article from his pocket*) I made a copy. It's a newspaper article.

EDNA   Oh. So you been thinkin' about it.

ANDREW Yeah.

EDNA Do you think about it a lot?

ANDREW Not a lot. But I think about it.

EDNA You were in bed. I remember that. Daddy wanted to go and I did, too. Morbid curiosity I guess. And people phonin'. You'd hang up and before you took a step, the phone'd be ringing again. I remember Tessa called—I don't know who else, but everybody was goin' it seemed like. Tessa and Ray were going, did we want to meet them? Did we know anybody stayin' there? We didn't know it at the time, but we did. Tim's sister-in-law, Milly, had a aunt there with her granddaughter. The both of 'em died. People saw 'em swept back by the smoke. The firemen were yellin' at them to jump—they had these nets to catch 'em, but they wouldn't or couldn't and the smoke covered them up. They were in this window and people saw 'em. Daddy said he saw 'em, but we didn't know who they were.

ANDREW I think I remember that, too.

EDNA You don't.

Andrew speaks simply, factually, more with specificity than emotion.

ANDREW But I do. This old lady and this little girl in this window wavin' and everybody yellin' at them, "jump, jump" and then they were gone. All this smoke and these white bedsheets hanging out the window, knotted together, dangling down all over the building with all this smoke.

EDNA You remember that? It's actual memory? It's not—you know how it happens sometimes, somebody tells you something.

ANDREW Well, can I say for sure? I don't know. But I sure think so.

EDNA Ain't that just terrible. I mean, that you remember it.

ANDREW People hanging on those white bedsheets. Other people jumping out of windows. I can see them in the air. And smoke everywhere. And yelling. I read here that one man jumped from the second floor into the net but his head hit the edge of the net, the ring part, and it's metal. Steel probably. He died. And a woman missed the net entirely and she died. And another man missed the net and went down an open manhole.

EDNA   Oh, my goodness.

ANDREW   Yeah. Right. An open manhole cover.

EDNA   People back then didn't know any better, Andrew. We just did things. I remember once hearing Dr. Laura on the radio one night, talking about something—it was similar but different, but it reminded me, and I got this feeling in the pit of my stomach, thinking back and I saw you the way Daddy had you on his shoulders and you were lookin' around at everything that was going on and it was like this storm and we were in the middle of it and I thought, Oh, boy, I bet we traumatized him.

ANDREW   I don't know about that.

EDNA   Sure. Look at it this way—all these years later, you're bringin' it up. You went down to the library and looked it up in the old newspapers. It's stuck in you somewhere. Don't you think?

ANDREW   I guess. Sure. I always wondered why you took me.

EDNA   We just wanted to go, and we couldn't very well leave you. I think we talked about it even. Maybe you'd just sleep through it all if we left you in your bed. But then what if you didn't? What if you woke up and nobody was there—the apartment was empty? Time was flyin', the phone ringin' off the hook, and Daddy was itchin' to go. So we took you. He run over to your little bed and grabbed you wrapped in your blanket and we ran down to the car. You didn't even wake up. He drove and I held you and you stayed sound asleep. Of course it was different once we got down to the fire.

beat

It's funny, though ain't it. The way some things just stick in a person. Sometimes I can't remember something I wanna remember, try as I might, and I think what's the point of even livin' your life since it all goes and you can't remember halfa what happened? Good things, sweet things. Then there's these other things, nasty things that stick— you want nothin' more to do with them, but you can't get rid of them no matter how you might think you want to.

ANDREW   Like what?

EDNA   Well, like you and the Whitfield fire, and you havin' parents dumb enough to drag you down there on purpose. Like that.

ANDREW   What about for you? I mean, in your case.

EDNA   Oh, there's stuff. There's plenty. Trust me. Nothin' big like you and that fire, but dumb little stuff like this once in Iowa City. Boy did I start thinkin' about that when we were down there.

ANDREW   Something happened in Iowa City?

EDNA   It goes way back. I woulda been twelve. You can see how long ago it was. Madeline was sixteen, and sick with the TB, and Mom was drivin' her down to Iowa City for some treatment or checkup. I was goin' along. I don't know why exactly. This was 1926 or so. So cars then and roads then, it was a long trip, and I don't remember much about the ride, but it was pouring rain when we got there. Mom got Madeline fixed up at the hospital, and then she told me I should go on over to the rooming house by myself. I'd been thinking we would stay together, Mom and me, the both of us at the rooming house, you know, a kind of sleepover, even though we were there for Madeline. But she told me she was going to stay in the hospital room so she could be close to Madeline. Sleep on the floor, if she had to. I went off in the pouring rain. It was night by then, dark, you know, pitch black except when the lightning lit things up, and I was twelve and all by myself. I was scared, I don't mind sayin' it. But I found my way, and they knew to let me in. I was soaked through and through, and cold, and I barely sat down in the room, when there was pounding on the door and when I asked, "Who's there?" it was Mom, just screamin',

"They wouldn't let me stay with her." She come in dripping and wailing. "Ohhhh god, they threw me out." She couldn't stop. I tried to help her. Tried to console her, but she wanted nothin' to do with me. Just sat there sobbin', until she fell asleep. Now ain't that dumb—to let something like that eat at you for over sixty years.

ANDREW I don't know.

EDNA (*suddenly scolding herself*) Well, I do. And it was a little bit self-centered, too. If you look at it a certain way. Poor Madeline was the sick one. (*but then she defends herself*) But there was more to it. Just a lot went on that didn't sit right. It was always that way. In Mom and Dad's eyes, she could do no wrong. And wrong is all she did. Not bein' sick—though who knows? A lot of her troubles could have come from the way she carried on. She drove 'em crazy. Many's the night she was out till the wee hours. Or she didn't come home at all. (*these never before spoken of events overtake her in a rush; every now and then it's like electricity jolts her*) I can see my Dad plain as day pacin' around, waitin' up for her. They'd tell us kids to go to bed, and poor little Buddy would stay put, but Tim and me, we'd sneak back out. She was just plain boy crazy, Maddy was. Anything in pants. Boy, man, older than her by twenty years—it didn't matter. She was fourteen when this was goin' on and the man could be—well there was one, he was thirty if he was a day. And this is back then. Tim and me would be peekin' through the bannister at the top of the stairs, scared to death, watchin' Dad pace around and whip that big leather razor strap he had in the air. Then Maddy would come in and Dad and her would start yellin', and Mom would be cryin' and then he'd start smackin' her. And I mean hard. But it did no good. And the men would come to the door even and Dad would have to chase them away, and they were younger than him and scary. And it just went on—she just kept at it. Men, men, men. And this one time I was sneakin' and watchin'—spyin' I guess. And I've lived to wish I'd never done it, let me tell you. Maybe I coulda been a better person, if I didn't know what I saw. But there was all this commotion up in Mom and Dad's bedroom, and the doctor had come rushing up the stairs, and Maddy was in there, and I knew it—the doctor and all this screamin' I was scared for her, you know, scared she was dyin' and I loved her, you know—my big sister—so I was hidin in the hall and I saw Mom come out the door and she had this little tiny baby, she was carryin no bigger than a bar of soap, like a baby of soap and she carried it in this dish like a little soap dish, you know, across the hall to the bathroom up there. So I guess you know what that was. And the priest came, too, later on, they called him to give her last rites, she was that close to dyin'. Do you mind me tellin' you this, Andrew? I just got this feelin' I gotta get it off my chest, and why not now. I feel like I done something wrong. Or maybe sayin' it's wrong. I think I thought, "None of that for me. I'm not doin' anything like that ever." Where Maddy was bad I would be good. I musta thought something like that, don't you think? I'm going to be the one they can count on. I'm going to be the steady one, the dependable one, the good one. I think I counted on it all commin' around one day when she would have to feel awful about it. But it was like none of it ever happened, as far as she was concerned, and she was just this princess. It was always that way. Whatever she did, wherever she lived, whoever she married, they had to always be the best, and we all had to say so. Knowin' what I did, where did she get the gall? The way she could act so high and mighty. You know that mean letter I tole you I got—well she really lit into me at the end, and the kicker was that all our troubles over the years were because I was jealous of her. I read that and I thought, the heck with that noise. But do you know what? I was jealous of her. All my life. I can see it now. But not of her shoes and houses and dining sets and sure as heck not her husbands, but of how Mom and Dad favored her. Especially Mom. I was the old dray horse and she was the high-strung filly. And when the time come that Dad was dead and Mom got sick and ended up in that old folks home, who was the only one still livin' here in town? Well that would be me. Tim was in Des Moines and Madeline in Cleveland, and poor Buddy so lost. Everybody scattered. So I was the one the nurses called if Mom needed something. I visited and sat with her. A glutton for punishment too dumb to read the writin' on the wall. I thought she'd look up one day and say, "Thank you Edna." But when she looked up, her expression so sly, so almost evil, all she had to say was, "I know what you're up to. I see right through you, Edna. You're after my money." I would sit at her bed and she would yell at me that I was just trying to get her money. As if she had any money. There wasn't any money. She could be so mean. The diabetes affected her mind sometimes.

beat

So when she died, you remember how you couldn't make it back for the funeral? Let me tell you, you can thank your lucky stars, because you would have been treated to one heck of a sight. The last night of her wake this big man in a nice dark suit come up to the coffin, kinda sneaky-like, makin' me suspicious, and then I realized it was finished, he was going to close the lid. Something came over me. That's what those murderers on TV say, when they can't explain why they did what they did. Well, somethin' came over me, and I was in the coffin with her before I knew it. Right on top of her, tryin' to climb all the way in, huggin' her, you know, hangin' on for dear life, and screamin' "No, no. Mom. Mom!" Like that, you know. Hysterical. That's what people tell me, just making a fool of myself. It all got to me, I guess, same way it did when Mom came back to that rooming house cryin' so awful because she had to stay with me that night in Iowa City.

ANDREW Well, sure.

EDNA I guess. (*harsh and scolding*) Well, that's enough of that (*but then she can't stop*) Mom and Dad would just give her anything. Had to mortgage the house and borrow money from Uncle Fritz to fix up the screen porch upstairs into a kind of sanitarium when the TB came back. They couldn't get enough of her. Me they had enough of from day one.

ANDREW Oh, Mom, c'mon, that's not true.

EDNA She was the queen bee. And I was the worker bee. Like Grandpa Hadley used to say because I was born on a Monday. "Oh, a little girl born on Monday. She came to do the laundry." And that was me all right. (*stopping herself finally, angrily*) That just about sums it up. It coulda been worse. You know, truth be told, I can't hardly see straight. (*rising*) I'm thinking maybe its past my bedtime.

ANDREW (*jumping up, hurrying to her*)   Mom, c'mon. Stay up with me a little.

EDNA   Oh, I don't know.

ANDREW   Let's at least see what's on the boob tube. Maybe watch a little.

As Actor One bounds into place.

ACTOR ONE   Come on, Edna.

As he turns on the TV, they settle into the recliners.

EDNA   Is that what you want?

ANDREW   Keep me company, Mom. Come on. We might find something.

ACTOR ONE   Look. Look, look!

EDNA   Oh, wait. Yeah.

ANDREW   You see somethin' you want to watch?

ACTOR ONE   Andrew, it's that John Wayne you saw as a kid.

ANDREW   Mom, I think we saw this together.

EDNA   Did we?

ACTOR ONE   John Wayne, Henry Fonda, and Ward Bond. One of their best.

ANDREW   John Wayne and Henry Fonda. What's the name? I know, but I can't—Darn.

EDNA   Me neither. I'm drawin' a blank.

ACTOR ONE   *Fort Apache.*

ANDREW   *She Wore a Yellow Ribbon.*

ACTOR ONE   No, it's *Fort Apache.*

ANDREW   *Fort Apache.* That's what it is.

EDNA   It was way back when. I know that. And Daddy was with us.

ANDREW   Yeah. The three of us.

ACTOR ONE   And here it is—I have it! That epic moment, that epic, mythical moment. Dawn. And the bugler summons running young men, the cavalry troops . . . (*as a bugle sounds*) . . . who form a long line on their sturdy mounts. Just as Colonel Thursday, who is Henry Fonda, gallops up and shouts, "Column of fours left. Hoooooo!" And George O'brien yells it, too. "Fours left." And then it's John Wayne as Captain York shouting, "Fours left. Hoooo." And the music starts, all bouncy and brave; (*music begins*) and the long line forms into a cavalry column of four horsemen abreast, as Colonel Thursday salutes and the men are singing: (*and she sings*) "How swift the hours did pass with the girl I left behind me." And Henry Fonda rides, and John Wayne and John Agar and Ward Bond and Victor McLaglen ride, as the women watch and worry and the music turns into, "She Wore a Yellow Ribbon." (*accompanying the music, she sings the melody*) Dum de dum, de dum de dum de dum dum.

EDNA   There's that "Yellow Ribbon" tune, Andrew. That must be why you thought it.

ANDREW   Right. Sure. (*singing*) "Around her neck, she wore a yellow ribbon." C'mon, Mom. You're the singer. (*singing*) "She wore it for her lover who was in the cavalry."

EDNA   "Around her neck, she wore a yellow ribbon."

EDNA & ANDREW (*sort of together*)   "She wore it for her lover who was in the cavalry."

ACTOR ONE   "She wore it for her lover who was in the cavalry."

Andrew and Edna sit in their chairs looking at Actor One, bathed in light.

And they ride into the wilderness where danger lurks. But still they go. Brave men, riding and ready, eager for adventure. (*singing softly*)

"Around her neck, she wore a yellow ribbon. She wore it for her lover who was in the cavalry."

The lights go black, only to quickly rise, surreal and drastic. Edna and Andrew sleep in their chairs; Actor One sleeps on the floor. ACTOR THREE is discovered seated on the TV shelves Actor One just occupied. He's dressed as a cavalry soldier, tattered and dusty, wearing boots, a sabre on his hip, a pistol, folded wings on his back. He stands and walks, looking around, his boot thudding as he passes Edna, and then turns to look down at her. After a beat, she stirs. Her eyes open and she sees him.

EDNA   And who might you be?

ACTOR THREE (*expecting her to welcome him*)   Are you ready?

EDNA   For what?

ACTOR THREE   To go.

EDNA   Go where?

ACTOR THREE   I'm an angel.

EDNA   You don't say. You coulda fooled me.

ACTOR THREE (*moving to kneel beside her and patiently explain*)   I have no wish to fool you, Edna. Are you ready?

EDNA   For what?

ACTOR THREE   To go.

EDNA   Go where?

ACTOR THREE   With me.

EDNA (*staring for a second*)   Are you a real angel?

ACTOR THREE   You have been praying and praying that I come to take you away.

EDNA   I been askin' for help. That's what I been askin' for.

ACTOR THREE   Are you ready?

EDNA   For what?

ACTOR THREE   To go.

EDNA (*rising*)   I wish you'd stop sayin' that.

ACTOR THREE   We can chat along the way, Edna. (*gesturing grandly*)
Let us go.

EDNA   Don't you hear one word I'm saying? Sure I'm sicka this and
that and I been complainin', but this is some kind of a mixup.

He takes hold of her arm, and she pulls away.

You just hold your horses there, Bub.

ACTOR THREE   Edna, please.

EDNA   And don't you think you can "Edna please" me. (*walking
away into the kitchen*) Don't you think you can sweet talk me into
doin' somethin' I ain't ready to do. I ain't goin.

*He snaps a long leather razor strap loudly in the air and Edna recoils in
pain, as if struck.*

Owwwww. (*as she is hit again*) What the heck you doin'? (*Trying to
get away around the kitchen table*) Wait a minute now. That's no way to
act. What got into you?

He follows her, striking again.

Owwww. Darn it. You stop it. I'm an old lady. (*again he strikes.*) Why
you doin' this to me? (*and again*) That hurts. You just stop. That ain't
funny. What the heck do you think you're doin'?

*As Actor Two, drawn by Edna's suffering, enters up left. He stands in
front of the recliners watching.*

ACTOR THREE (*furious*)   I am getting you ready. You said you
weren't ready. I am getting you ready. (*hitting her*)

EDNA   Owwwww. Stop it now. Please. This ain't right. (*seeing
Andrew asleep in the arm chair*) Andrew. Look at what he's doin'. Make

him stop. (*struck again*) Owwww. Owwww. That hurts. It really does. It hurts awful. Andrew.

ACTOR THREE   He can't do anything.

EDNA (*sinking to the floor*)   Just stop. Stop. Okay, okay. I give up.

ACTOR THREE   Are you saying you're ready? (*striking again*)

EDNA   I'll do it. I'm ready. I'll go. (*looking up at him*) Just stoppit, darn you.

ACTOR THREE   I have. I've stopped.

EDNA   Just my luck I'd get a mean one.

ACTOR THREE   We are all the same.

EDNA   I sure hope not.

ACTOR THREE (*compassionate, he crouches to soothe her*)   You have to leave the earth, Edna, and misery makes you want to go. The day, the epoch, the hour, century, month, year, and instant of your departure has arrived. And so I visit to make you miserable.

EDNA   Some job you got.

ACTOR THREE   It's not my job. It's my being.

Shifting, Edna sees Actor Two standing there.

EDNA   Don't you look so smug. I mean, you better believe you're goin', too. That's right, you dirty thing. It's all your fault.

ACTOR TWO   What is?

EDNA   Oh, don't act stupid. You're going with me!

ACTOR TWO   I want to go with you. I must always be with you. (*moving the join Actor Three and assist Edna to her feet*) Where are we going?

EDNA   I don't know where we're goin'. (*suddenly anguished*) I really don't know. I don't. (*to Actor Three*) What if you're not even really an angel?

ACTOR THREE   Edna, what else could I be?

EDNA   But how'm I supposed to know? Unless maybe . . . (*patting her head*) You hit me hard. I'm feelin' a little dreamy. You keep sayin', "Let us go." Am I actually going somewhere with you?

ACTOR TWO   Edna, my darling, my dear one, talk to me. Talk to me.

EDNA   Why should I? You're not my friend. The heck with you. (*back to Actor Three*) Let's go if we're going. Can we go?

Because Actor Three blocks the way, Actor Two cannot move to her, and so he reaches for her.

ACTOR TWO   Edna, my beloved. Take my hand.

EDNA   No, I will not. I'm done with you. This is where you and me part ways. (*headed for the door, she sees Andrew*) Ohh, look at Andrew, sleeping like a baby. Bye Andrew, bye bye.

As Edna reaches the door, Actor Three moves as her protector.

ACTOR TWO   But we can't part ways, Edna. I can't live without you.

EDNA   Well, you shoulda thought of that sooner. Because it's over for me, and when it's over for me, it's over for you. How come you never thought of that, if you're so darn smart?

Edna goes.

ACTOR TWO   Edna, wait! Please!

Actor Three raises his sword silencing Actor Two, who falls to his knees.

ACTOR THREE (*advancing*)   In the name of Holy Mary, Mother of God, Queen of Heaven and Earth, Star of the Sea, and in the name of Saint Peregrine, we condemn you. We cast you down to dirt and slime. We abandon you. We leave you behind.

Actor Three slashes with his sabre annihilating Actor Two who cries out as light, sound, deliver this otherworldly happening into darkness. Then Andrew is found sleeping in his recliner, the other recliner empty. Actor One kneels in front of him. She tugs at his pant leg, before speaking.

ACTOR ONE I'm on, Andrew. You left me on all night. So I'm just sitting here all night, playing one random thing after another—just on and on—whatever comes up. I'm just—

ANDREW Ohhhh, wow. Mom? Mommy . . . ? *(waking befuddled, looking around at the empty room.)*

ACTOR ONE She's gone. You were watching a movie and—

ANDREW Right, right. We started that movie. *The Searchers* or . . . John Wayne. No, not *The Searchers.*

ACTOR ONE *Fort Apache.*

ANDREW *(rising, half asleep)* What?

ACTOR ONE *Fort Apache.* And there's another John Wayne starting on channel 36, I'd like you to know; *Red River,* one they don't show very often.

Edna appears in her room; she wears a robe and paces uneasily.

ANDREW Now? *(moving toward Edna's door, carrying the remote)*

ACTOR ONE Can you believe it? A Howard Hawks classic. Introducing Montgomery Clift. A young John Wayne. Walter Brennan.

ANDREW I don't think I can. *(shutting off the TV)*

ACTOR ONE But you love *Red River.* You always say it's the greatest of all the John Wayne movies ever.

ANDREW Mom? Mommy. . . . ? *(rapping gently at Edna's door)*

EDNA Is that you, Andrew?

ANDREW Yes, it is. You in there?

EDNA Where else would I be?

ANDREW   Are you okay?

EDNA   Did you want something?

ANDREW   Just checking.

EDNA   On what?

ANDREW   I just wanted to say hi. I woke up in the chair. I guess you got up earlier.

EDNA   Lemme put on my glasses.

ANDREW   No, don't get up. It's the middle of the night. Sorry. Go back to sleep if you can. I'm going to bed now. I think I had a bad dream.

EDNA   Did you now? It must be goin' around. Because I had one, too.

ANDREW   No kidding. What was it?

EDNA   Don't ask me. Woke me up but then it was gone.

ANDREW   Mine, too. I can't remember any of it.

EDNA   Darn things.

ANDREW   Anyway, here we are—happy to have left our bad dreams behind and found each other safe and sound in your little apartment.

EDNA   That's a good way to put it.

ANDREW   Sorry I woke you. 'Night then.

EDNA   'Night.

ANDREW (*moving toward his room*)   See you in the morning.

As the lights go to black.

Scene v

Morning. Edna walks out of her room and goes to the kitchen where she turns on the stove. She takes a pot from the refrigerator and places it on the stove. The door opens and Andrew hurries in with a newly purchased gym bag.

ANDREW   Hi. I didn't take too long, did I?

EDNA   Not at all. Did you find everything you wanted?

ANDREW (*rushing into his room*)   Sure did.

EDNA   They keep things pretty well stocked over there, I find. They're a pretty good little drugstore. Was it crowded?

Coming out with his suitcase, he places it near the front door and heads into the bathroom.

ANDREW   Not too.

EDNA   Who was on the register?

ANDREW   Big woman. Blonde.

EDNA   That's that Doris. Tried to talk your ear off, I bet.

Moving about, he gathers his computer case, his Dopp kit with his suitcase near the door.

ANDREW   I couldn't make up my mind about which bag I wanted. And she was pretty helpful.

EDNA   You better eat this little bit before it gets cold. What time's that cab gettin' here? Pretty quick, I would guess.

ANDREW   Well, ten minutes or so.

EDNA   Lord, you better eat quick then.

At the kitchen table, Andrew picks up the two photo albums.

ANDREW   You're sure about this? You want me to take both albums.

EDNA   Yes, I do. And see that Jenny gets one.

ANDREW (*zippering open the new gym bag, he packs the albums*)   Sorry about the zipper.

EDNA (*watching him, she moves to the flowers on the table*)   I been lookin' at these flowers and I think they're done for. What do you say?

ANDREW   You could keep them a while longer, if you wanted.

EDNA   That's the thing of it, though. I don't know what I want. Why'd you think I asked you?

ANDREW   Well, sure.

EDNA   Well, sure what?

ANDREW   I'm thinking.

EDNA   About what? That's one thing I got to say. What are you thinking about? I never know. Half the time I couldn't even venture a guess.

ANDREW   Well, about the flowers at the moment. About what you should do.

EDNA   So do you have an opinion? Or does it have the both of us stumped?

ANDREW   Well, they don't stink. Strong smell, but . . .

EDNA   But they're drooping. No denying that one. Droopy and gettin ready to stink. Like me, wouldn't you say?

ANDREW   Oh, Mom.

EDNA   Oh, Mom, what?

ANDREW   You know.

EDNA   Well, that's easy to say. You try walkin' around with a bag of this dirty stuff on you. See what your nose makes of it. Nothin' pretty let me tell you. You remember that big Christmas party at your place last year? Was it last year? And I started to stink.

ANDREW (*placing the gym bag with the other bags near the door*) That was last year. You weren't there the year before.

EDNA Wasn't I?

ANDREW No. Last year for sure.

EDNA And the bag's gotta start to leak right when I'm at the dinner table. Oh, my god I don't even like thinkin' about it. That was just awful. I just hated it. A person takes pride in bein' clean and then something like that happens.

ANDREW You couldn't help it.

EDNA Of course not. But what does that matter? It happened. I didn't even notice at first. Until I saw that nice boy—he was so nice to me, sat across the table and talked to me just like I was a regular person—

ANDREW Richard Nolan.

EDNA Yes. That's it. That nice Richard Nolan started sniffin' the air. That's when I caught on. I saw him sniffin' and I sniffed and oh my god, it hit me like a ton of bricks. I smell like poop. I took off like my chair was on fire.

ANDREW I remember.

EDNA Do you?

ANDREW I didn't know what happened.

EDNA I was runnin' for my life. Mortified. Just mortified. I'd a liked to jumped in a hole and pulled it in after me. Got upstairs and my dress had poop all on the side. I was scared I'd maybe dripped on my chair.

ANDREW No. That didn't happen. I ran up to the guest room to check if you didn't feel well or what, remember? And you told me what happened so I ran back and checked the chair. But it was okay.

EDNA Well, thank goodness for small favors. No poop on my chair. Just on my dress.

ANDREW Nobody noticed.

No matter what he says, she demands that he confirm how awful the event was.

EDNA Nobody except that poor Richard Nolan. Probably thought somebody farted.

ANDREW Maybe. But no idea who.

EDNA He hadda think somethin' and that was better than the truth. It was a terrible dumb business. That's all I know. I'm gonna toss these flowers out. That's my decision. Unless you stand opposed.

ANDREW I think it's up to you.

EDNA Okay then. Out they go.

Marching to the waste, she dumps the flowers, while Andrew drags the second recliner to the corner where it was when he arrived. Edna turns to watch him.

Where'd you say Angela was going?

ANDREW This camp. It's a wilderness camp. They go to class and everything but—

EDNA How long will she be gone? Because let me tell you something—sometimes your kids go away, and they don't come back.

ANDREW Meaning me . . . I guess?

EDNA If the shoe fits. You think you'll have a family, and it'll be sweet and good, you and your kids, and it'll all be nice, but then things happen—your kids get sick and you're scared, and other things happen—you do things, like we did, not knowin' any better. Thinkin' its the right thing when you oughta know it's not. But there's some stuff, it just gets in and it stays. Like us dragging you to that fire. Once I heard that program with Dr. Laura, I can't tell you how many times I wished I could take it back. Do you think about it a lot?

ANDREW   No. Not at all.

EDNA   But you do think about it. You have to. Goin' to the library and all, the way you did. Do you think we did you harm?

ANDREW   I'm fine, Mom.

EDNA   Oh, sure. You're successful as all get out—you're doin' fine—nice family, big house, but still. You're just a poor little guy and we drag you down there. And neither one of us has the good sense to think maybe it's not right, you bein' there. It's a cryin' shame. You musta thought you were looking at Hell. That's how it musta looked to you—all that fire and smoke and people fallin'—those white sheets hanging—that's how it musta seemed. Hell. You think that's behind some of the troubles we had?

ANDREW   What? No, no. That's all in the past.

EDNA   We had our troubles, Andrew, you and me and Daddy.

ANDREW   I know. You don't have to *tell* me.

EDNA   It's no good to sweep it all under the rug. Dr. Laura says these things gotta be talked out if you get the chance.

ANDREW   It's all fine, Mom.

A car horn honks outside.

EDNA   Is that him? It can't be him.

ANDREW   He's a little early.

Both go to the big window to look out.

Looks like it, Mom. (*hurrying to his bags*)

EDNA   Okay, okay. I know you been good to me. Don't think I forgot about that. I tell everybody I can. Good as you were to us both when Daddy was still alive, I ought to know not to worry. Sendin' money the way you did—the way you still do every month. Regular as clockwork. I'd bring in the mail to Daddy because he—

ANDREW   It wasn't that much, Mom.

EDNA   It was plenty and we couldn't have done without it. It made all the difference.

Honking outside.

Darn him. Can't he wait?

He moves to her, hugging her; she clings to him.

Ohh, that feels so good. I can't tell you.

ANDREW (*patting her, moving off*)   Gotta go, Mommy.

EDNA   Okay, okay. But that other stuff is all behind us now. That's what you're saying.

ANDREW   Of course it is, Mom. You know that.

She follows him partway to the door, where he picks up his bags.

EDNA   I don't. Sometimes I worry. You're so far away and I don't hear from you.

ANDREW   I always tell you, if I don't call, then you call me. Pick up the phone and call. Any time.

EDNA   I guess I want to be remembered, Andrew. If you call, then I know you were thinking of me. I don't want to feel I'm buttin' in.

ANDREW   You're not. You wouldn't be.

More honking, as she looks to the window and back at him.

EDNA   It's always this way. I got all this stuff to say, all these questions to ask, and I don't get to it. And then off you go.

ANDREW   We'll see each other soon, Mom. I'll get back.

EDNA Say what you want, Andrew, there were troubles. We were a family. I could kick myself for that fire business and maybe a couple dozen other dumb things we did to you and Jenny, too. Even though we always meant well. I mean, Daddy loved you kids. You know that. And he meant well. But things didn't go the way they should have in his life, the way he hoped. He had a lot of disappointments and a lot of frustrations, and he could lose his temper, so he hit you in ways he shouldn't but I know he loved you. We were all handsy in those days. I hit you, I was way too quick with my hands. Just give you a slap in the face. And spankings. The both of you when you were little. But we thought that was what you did. We thought it was right. Do you remember any of that?

ANDREW (*bags slung and picked up, he reaches for the door*) I really better go, Mom. That driver's liable to get fed up and take off without me.

EDNA Do you slap your kids?

ANDREW What?

EDNA Do you?

ANDREW Why are you asking me now?

EDNA Because I want to know.

ANDREW We can talk on the phone. I'll call you.

EDNA I bet you don't, do you.

ANDREW No.

EDNA Never.

ANDREW No.

EDNA Not even once. None of them.

ANDREW No. I never have.

EDNA Oh, that just makes me sick. I swear. (*she flees toward the recliner*) Not that you don't hit your kids. Don't think that. I'm glad you don't. But that we did it. But people back then were different. I know I said that, but it's true. Not that it's an excuse.

ANDREW (*leaving his bags, he goes to where she sits*)   Mom, none of that bothers me. It doesn't.

EDNA   You're sure.

ANDREW   Yes.

EDNA   Don't hate me, Andrew. (*heartbroken*)

ANDREW   What? Mom! No, no.

EDNA   It's all behind us. Don't hate me. You're sure. Cause now'd be the time, if it wasn't.

ANDREW   It's all behind us.

EDNA   Because I talked to Doctor Spencer.

ANDREW   What?

EDNA   And everything's the way it was. It's all like they been tellin' us. My destiny and all. There's no hope. Nothin' to be done.

Andrew stands stunned. And then he turns out to the audience.

ANDREW   I didn't go. (*crossing down front*) I went out and talked to the cab driver. I paid him in full. Apologized. Gave him a good tip. And then three days later another cab with a different driver took me to the airport and I flew out of town. I had to. Work. Kids. Dogs. Marriage. You know. Life. (*after a glance at her*) Over the next months, we talked on the phone. For the most part, she seemed okay, and she insisted she was fine. Jenny went out for a visit. And then one night the phone rang. Mom was crying. She had stubbed her toe. It was the last straw. That little pain on top of all else. She was crying like one of my kids. "I can't take it any more," she said. "Walking around this stupid apartment alone in the dark. I'm just a big clumsy dummy banging into things. I'm sick, Andrew. I felt myself changing over these last days. I'm sick and I'm scared." I tried to console her; I said Jenny or I would come out right away. I'd been in bed when the phone rang. I'd come down stairs to talk so my wife could sleep and so I wouldn't disturb the kids in their bedrooms nearby. I was sitting in the dark, and there was a big window full of night sky where the moon seemed full, though I couldn't see it. Just the white power of the light, as I sat listening to her say, "I wish you were here now."

beat

I couldn't leave immediately but Jenny went the next day. When I arrived a few days later, Mom was already in the hospital and I'd come down with a terrible cold. It made me want to keep my distance. I explained that I didn't want to give her my cold and have it turn into pneumonia or something—bronchitis—and so I sat on the opposite side of the room. My voice was hoarse—I could barely make myself heard. "What are you looking at?" she said this once. I was staring at her. I didn't know. I hurried close, kissed her brow and went back to my chair. I told myself I was on the other side of the room because of my cold and that was true. But there was another kind of distance involved. Our distance. Jenny stayed on and so we were both there when a few days later they wanted to put a port in to give her morphine and we said "yes," and when she went down to surgery we said, "See you soon," with no idea that these were going to be among the last words we'd say to her and be sure she understood and knew who we were. When she came up from surgery, the nurses asked if she wanted a blanket, and she said, "Yes, a pretty one." Not long after that the drug took her off. Once when I came in with coffee from the cafeteria Jenny was brushing Mom's hair. She wanted her to look pretty. She was crying and told me none of the nurses knew who Mom really was. How smart and sharp and funny. Once I went close and asked her a question, and she said, "Yes please." And then she said, "Thank you father," thinking I was a priest, I guess.

beat

The morning she died, I'd spent the night in her room sleeping on a cot. We were in hospice by then, and she was breathing hard all night. The nurses came in, changing sheets, shifting her around, these shadow shapes, like intruders. In the morning, Jenny came to sit with her. We were alternating nights. I headed back to the apartment for a quick shower. The phone rang almost the instant I opened the apartment door. A nurse told me to hurry back. I ran to the car and I drove quickly, but I did not get there on time. My sister said she thought maybe Mom didn't want to die in front of me, and that she waited until I was gone.

beat

Don't you wonder where they go? I do. I wasn't with Mom, but I've seen others. We're there. With them, we think. It seems we are. And their eyes have a veiled gaze, an inward gaze, like they're looking into something, but doctors say it's just a fading of function, and it could be only that. But it could be looking into something, too. That the fading of physical function opens the way. That our whole relation with this world that we love so much is in the way—a veil that keeps us from seeing, and as it fades, as function fails we see something else. And there's a breath, and then another. Another. One more. And then the last. It's clear that something happened. The difference is obvious. There's no mistaking the change. They're dead we say. He's dead. She's dead. But we don't know what we saw. Where they go. Or if they go. I don't anyway.

beat

But before all that—before that last visit ended—

EDNA   Andrew. What The heck you doin'?

ANDREW (*startled*)   What?

EDNA   Didn't you hear me? Just off in the clouds. I asked you a question. Since you're staying on a bit more, I thought we might see about getting to that movie. It sounds good.

ANDREW   You think so? Sure. Tonight?

EDNA   Just off in another world, weren't you. You've been that way as far back as I can remember. Always getting lost in one daydream or another. Playing cowboys like you thought you could grow up and be one. Go back in time.

ANDREW   Mom, I was just thinking.

EDNA   Or that darn telescope. What was that all about anyway?

ANDREW   What telescope?

EDNA   Andrew. Don't tell me you don't remember. You were little. We were in the little apartment. You were maybe eight. All of a sudden you had to have a telescope. Kinda desperate even. You gotta remember.

ANDREW   I don't. Sorry.

EDNA   We didn't have two nickels to rub together to buy you one. But then you discovered this advertisement where you could send away for one with box tops and a little money. So you collected all these box tops and saved up your allowance and sent it all off. Every day from then on you come runnin' home from school straight to the mailbox to see if it was there. Don't you remember any that?

ANDREW   Oh, my goodness. (*starting to remember*)

EDNA   I can see you clear as a bell the day it finally came. The instructions said you should use a cardboard toilet paper roll from the bathroom for your telescope. And you're all bent over at that little kitchen table we had back then with this toilet paper roll, just like they told you, and you're gluing in these things they sent. Looked like ice cubes, only round . . . like paraffin lids. Lenses, I guess they were, and when you looked through them, I looked, too. We both looked.

ANDREW   And it was like looking into a bucket of snow. Mom, I'd forgotten all about that.

EDNA   And then sittin' at that poor old kitchen table when you saw what you had and finally gave up, you burst into tears. I couldn't see a dang thing up in the sky, but I could see that. I could see you.

ANDREW   How could I have forgotten? (*going deep into thought to remember*)

EDNA   What do you think you were hoping to see? The moon? The stars, what else? Heaven, maybe? (*watching, waiting*) Andrew? Lord, when I see you startin' to daydream that way I gotta wonder what you're thinkin' about.

ANDREW   It doesn't matter.

EDNA   Yes, it does. And self-centered though it may be, I can't help but ask myself if there's anything I could do that would interest you in me half as much as whatever you're thinkin' about.

ANDREW   Mom, c'mon.

EDNA   No, I do. I have often asked myself that question.

ANDREW   Mom, I was just thinking.

EDNA   But I'm serious, Andrew. I want to know. What do you think? Is there anything that I could ever do that would get your attention and keep it?

Pause

Well, is there?

She sits quietly. He watches her and then turns to the audience.

ANDREW   And so she did it, don't you see? One minute she was there and then it was like I looked away, and when I looked back . . . she was gone.

MUSIC: Lights go out on him and then on her.

END OF PLAY

Good for Otto

David Rabe

Based On Material from
Undoing Depression by Richard O'Connor

For those who do the work.

PRODUCTION CREDITS

The world premiere of *Good for Otto* was produced and presented by the Gift Theater in October 2015. It was directed by Michael Patrick Thornton, the set was by Courtney O'Neil, the costume design was by Stephanie Cluggish, the lighting design was by Charles Cooper, the sound design and original music was by Christopher Kriz, and the stage manager was Corinne James.

The cast was as follows:

MARCY	Cyd Blakewell
MOM	Brittany Burch
TIMOTHY	John Connolly
JIMMY	Paul D'Addario
TERESA	Patricia Donegan
DR. MICHAELS	John Gawlik
FRANNIE	Caroline Heffernan
JANE	Alexandra Main
MRS. GARLAND	Donna McGough
JEROME	Kenny Mihlfried
NORA	Darci Nalepa
EVANGELINE RYDER	Lynda Newton
BARNARD	Rob Riley
DENISE	Justine Serino
ALEX	Jay Worthington

CHARACTERS

DR. MICHAELS—a therapist in his midforties.

JEROME—a patient in his thirties.

MOM—a figure in her early thirties.

JANE—a patient in her forties.

JIMMY—Jane's son in his late twenties, early thirties.

MRS. GARLAND—Jerome's mother—in her late forties

EVANGELINE—a therapist in her early forties.

TIMOTHY— a patient in his late forties, early fifties.

FRANNIE—a patient, twelve years old.

NORA—early thirties, a foster mom hoping to adopt Frannie.

DENISE—secretary in her midthirties.

TERESA—married to Barnard, seventies.

BARNARD—a patient in his seventies.

MARCI—an insurance company case manager in her thirties.

ALEX—a patient in his early thirties.

The play takes place in a theatrical space that is sometimes literally a Mental Health Center, at other times it's a surreal space, Dr. Michaels's psyche or imagination.

ACT ONE

Set: the main playing area holds two office chairs on wheels positioned toward the center while a piano stands along one side. A pile of books, a stack of folders, a bottle of bourbon, and several glasses stand atop the piano. A door, the entrance from the hall outside and reception area of the Mental Health Center occupies the opposite side with two chairs to indicate a waiting room.

There are five stations around the main playing area. Each contains furniture that defines the characters who will occupy them. JIMMY and JANE in one. JEROME in another. FRANNIE and NORA another. BARNARD and TERESA in another. And MOM alone and elevated.

At the start, the characters enter and go to their stations. The last to arrive is DR. MICHAELS, who looks things over, and then hums a note, or perhaps plays a note on a pitch pipe. All the characters join with him in humming a wordless, harmonious note. They settle in their places, and he addresses the audience:

DR. MICHAELS The Town of Harrington sits near the Berkshire Mountains and along the Mohegan river. There are numerous lakes and ponds. Open fields, wooded areas, and farmlands are plentiful, and the mountains harbor abundant, picturesque hiking trails with names like Owl Mountain, and the Arrowhead Trail. We have a Congregational church, an Episcopal, Methodist, Baptist, and Catholic, and a Jewish Temple just across the New York state line.

beat

Now. Imagine me in bed, if you will, on a morning just before dawn, any morning, an average morning. Imagine me awake thinking, hoping for a little more sleep. Imagine a blue down comforter, a late fall day. I live fairly close to the Northwood Mental Health Center,

111

where I am a counselor and chief administrator. It's a short drive, or a pleasant walk, if I'm not too busy which isn't often. We see a great many people in the community, but others who could benefit refuse to come by, or don't know we exist, and many of those who do come are embarrassed. They take precautions not to be seen leaving our doors. That's what I'm thinking about laying there. Because in spite of the bucolic countryside, in spite of the sky, the trails, the lakes, pain is plentiful here. Twenty-first century Americans in the land of plenty. But there's money problems; family and work pressure. Autism. O.C.D. Alcohol and drug abuse, sexual abuse. Being young. Getting old. It all sits hidden in our little world of bright skies, bright lakes and tall trees. And then finally, of course, there's simply and always the problem of being human.

Jerome calls from his setting of piled up boxes.

JEROME   I have all these boxes, Dr. Michaels. I don't know how many. A great number of boxes. A great number of very important boxes . . . (*taking out a strange, random object*) . . . because in these boxes are the projects for my future.

DR. MICHAELS (*to Jerome*)   I know you're having trouble with all the boxes, Jerome, and I'm thinking hard about what we can do to help you. I promise. But our appointment isn't until ten thirty, and I'm not fully awake. So you understand if I haven't figured it out yet. I haven't even had my coffee. I'm actually still in bed.

JEROME   But there seem to be more boxes. More and more. The piles are getting higher.

DR. MICHAELS   That's not possible Jerome, unless you're adding boxes. Are you adding boxes, Jerome?

JEROME   I didn't add many.

DR. MICHAELS (*back to the audience*)   I wake early most mornings with the sun pawing at the edge of the drawn blinds, and lying there in that twilight of neither sleep nor complete wakefulness, I sometimes see my dead mother, her eyes fixed on me with an enormous, questioning look.

Mom stands in faint light looking down on him. She's young, as she would have been when he was nine.

Or sometimes in the middle of the night she's floating outside in the dark air, which appears quite detailed with moonlight, stars—though, as I said, the blinds are closed. She committed suicide when I was nine years old.

MOM   And yet I am always near. Robert.

DR. MICHAELS   That's not really her.

MOM   It is, too.

DR. MICHAELS   No, Mom. You're long dead. Long gone.

MOM   Then why are you talking to me?

DR. MICHAELS   You're a thought. A memory. I'm thinking. That's all.

MOM   Look at me and say that.

DR. MICHAELS   You're not there. You niggle in my thoughts. Nose around, poking in and out to insinuate your points, sometimes in your own name, but at other times anonymously, or . . . pretending to be me. But you're not really there. I don't actually see you.

JEROME (*somewhat assertive*)   We have got to do something about all the boxes, Dr. Michaels! So I can move into my new apartment.

DR. MICHAELS   I know, Jerome. It's important and I got a little distracted. But it's only about six hours until our appointment and we'll work on it then.

JEROME   It's five hours and seventeen minutes, Dr. Michaels.

DR. MICHAELS (*to the audience, his back to Jerome*)   Jerome lives with his mother and step-father. His real dad ran off when Jerome was small. He wasn't as smart as Jerome, I suspect, and so Jerome got a beating or two.

JEROME (*interrupting*)   Dr. Michaels?

DR. MICHAELS Yes.

JEROME What are you thinking about?

DR. MICHAELS Well . . . , you, Jerome.

JEROME Are you really thinking of me? Really?

DR. MICHAELS Yes. About how to help you.

JEROME Now? Right now?

DR. MICHAELS Yes.

JEROME And before that?

DR. MICHAELS Yes. A little bit.

JEROME Are you always thinking of helping me, Dr. Michaels? Always?

DR. MICHAELS Not always.

Distant gunshot. Everyone looks. Jane and Jimmy sit side by side, both in work clothes, Jane in a baseball cap, as she addresses the audience.

JANE Whenever I think of Jimmy, I get this terrible headache. It's terrible. I mean, not with every thought of him, but it feels like it. It feels hard and dangerous to think of him and so I don't want to do it, but of course I do want to think about him. Because he was my son, and I knew he was in trouble off and on, but he was thirty-four, you know. I mean, a grown up and he'd been a troublemaker and had a few arrests, but all minor stuff. Sometimes he didn't live with me, but stayed with friends. But on this night, he was living with me, and he came home late. It was about midnight. Just a little past midnight and I got out of bed when I heard him and went out in my pajamas, because I had to get up to go to work at six in the morning—he was reading a motorcycle magazine, sitting on the couch with a beer. I could see the photographs of the engine part of this big black motorcycle, and I asked him if he needed anything and he said no. He seemed his regular self, as far as I could tell, but I stood looking at him for a few seconds, watching him turn the page, and then he looked up at me and he—he looked right at me and he said—

JIMMY (*looking at her*)   I'm fine, Mom. You go back to bed. You look tired.

JANE   Okay.

JIMMY   'Night, Mom.

JANE   Good night, Jimmy. (*pause*) So I went back to bed and he got up at some point and went into his bedroom and shot himself in the head while I was sleeping. In the room right next door.

JIMMY   I was fine, as far as I knew. I was drunk, a little, and you know some shit had happened. But when doesn't it. There's always shit of one kind or another. I don't think I was thinking about anything special or unusual, but just going to bed until I saw the shotgun in the corner. It stopped me in my tracks is the way I would put it. It was like it spoke almost, called out from the corner, "Hey, I'm over here; don't forget about me."

JANE   I learned later that he'd been drinking quite a bit, and that at the local hangout earlier in the evening he'd run into his ex-wife, Susie, and that when he went up to her and tried to talk Susie had gone out of her way to be really snotty to him. That's the report I got. "Susie was really snotty to him." So Jimmy had left the bar to get away from his snooty ex-wife and had gone to a different bar in the hopes of—I don't know what—fun, or a chance to drink in peace, and who does he run into there but his idiot father who was totally shit-faced. Just stupefied. I say "stupefied" because an eyewitness to their encounter told me that Marty, my ex-goddamn-husband was so drunk he didn't even recognize Jimmy at first. He didn't even understand that this nice young man who'd come up to him and was talking—that it was his own son. So as far as bars were concerned that was two for two in the bad luck department for Jimmy. I guess he came home not long after that. When he looked up and told me he was fine and said "Good night" I was tired and had to get up at six and I didn't know any of this stuff that had happened, and I went to bed.

Having left his area, Jimmy wanders the main playing area.

JIMMY So I'm undressing; the beer empty, the gun in the corner talking. But I'm going to get some sleep, and dream maybe about the motorcycle engine I'd been reading about. The thing about a motorcycle—which I love to ride them—is the speed and the wind in your face and the way it just blows your thoughts right out of your head, the noise of it in your ears, or even magnified bigger and bigger by the ear holes in the helmet if you're wearing a helmet, and it's like this wind going into your brain and through your brain, just taking your thoughts out and carrying them away. I only got about halfway undressed and I was sitting on the bed and I was tired and feeling sort of dead already, in a way, or dead tired, and the shotgun was there. My idiot father—what a joke, and I was trying to laugh, the way his eyes had looked at me, these big blank circles that couldn't quite get a fix on me, or were focused like I was some very faraway distant object, and he didn't know what I was, exactly, let alone who. I was like some vague TV face he'd seen on some show somewhere. Then this fat guy came up and ridiculed my idiot dad about how he didn't even know his own son. "What?" he says. So the guy slobbers all over us both telling us one more time, who we are and good ole idiot dad comes around to face me and you can see the channel changer somewhere in behind his eyes go click-click and like now I'm maybe in color and he says, "Jimmy! Hey, Kid, gimme twenty dollars. Now!" I give him ten. And Susie, when I think about her, when I come up to her, just to say "hi"—that's all.

He looks up at Mom who, in half-light seems Susie.

Nothin' more. I just got sad looking across that fucked-up bar and seeing her and it don't seem right, and all I want to say when I go over is "Hello. How you doin'?" I mean, we were a love story . . . of some half-assed kind. But she's gotta be nasty. What for? She's gotta be a sly little bitch to me. For what? She kind of snorts and huffs, and wrinkles her lip. What's it going to get her? Can anybody tell me? I don't get it. Why do people have to be that way? Anyway, I'm in the room. My shotgun's there. My big ole twelve gauge.

And the gun is there, hovering in the air handed down to him by Mom.

It's talking. I'm not talking. Nobody else is talking. Just the gun. I'd picked it up a hundred times. And so it was nothing, picking it up again. By then I knew, of course, or had some idea—because I'd written the note—I put the barrel to my head—that wasn't hard—seemed sort of ordinary, totally ordinary—I mean, it didn't hurt or anything and I pointed it right here to that spot in between your eyes. Like if there's some third eye like people joke about, then that's my target. I'm thinking, if I've picked this damn thing up once, I've picked it up a thousand times. It was little or nothing to do it again. I'd picked it up and shot things all my life. So I picked it up one more time and shot myself. Oh, shit, I thought. It was like, it was like, it was like going down the drain. Or into this big roaring vacuum cleaner. The wind in my ears. A ride on the fastest, scariest motorcycle that I rode right out of everything.

Jane strides out to sit in one of the chairs facing Dr. Michaels, seated in the other chair.

JANE The suicide note which he left was really more of a half-baked last will and testament. What it consisted of was instructions about what should happen to a few of his things. I read it and then I read it again and I kept looking for some little touch of feeling, of love or unhappiness or regret. Or maybe a reason. But it was just this list. There was nothing more there no matter how often I read it. He wanted his brother to have his motorcycle and he had this collection of baseball cards he wanted to give to a neighbor kid. And he wanted his brother to have the shotgun. The very Remmington shotgun he used. What was he thinking? I put my foot down. I threw that damn gun in the lake.

DR. MICHAELS When this happens, Jane, when a loved one takes their life, and you're left behind, there's a sense that you're guilty and—

JANE   But I should have seen something. Known to sit up with him.

DR. MICHAELS   You had no idea what was going to happen.

As Mom walks in to join and watch.

JANE (*rubbing her head*)   I'm his mother. It was there and I missed it. Or I saw it and didn't know what it was.

DR. MICHAELS   Is your head hurting now?

JANE   Yes. Yes. It's really so . . . just . . . wow.

DR. MICHAELS   Where did Jimmy shoot himself?

JANE   What? Well . . . (*touching her head*) Yes, I know, I know. Here. (*looking intently at him*) I'm not doing this on purpose.

DR. MICHAELS   Of course not. But if it's a psychosomatic symptom mimicking his injury, it could be a kind of sharing, a way of staying close to him.

JANE   It hurts is what I know. Why didn't he just say something? And why in my house? It feels personal—like he meant something about me.

DR. MICHAELS   I can't pretend to know what was in Jimmy's mind that night, but —

JANE   So what good are you?

Rising, she strides off leaving Mom and Dr. Michaels.

MOM   Do you think Jane will be next? That you'll pick up the paper and read in the police report that Jane Drysdale died by her own hand? Maybe she didn't actually throw that shotgun in the lake, like she said, but is keeping it for a rainy day.

DR. MICHAELS   Right. Where's my crystal ball? (*rising, crossing to the piano for a drink*)

MOM   You should have helped that poor Jimmy.

DR. MICHAELS   I didn't even know him.

MOM   It must be so hard—knowing that you can't stop us all—the kid who told a friend he's thinking of killing himself. Or the misfit who wrote an essay that made a teacher worry.

DR. MICHAELS   If we get a call, we do something about it.

MOM   But you can't spot us all. You know how good at hiding we are. Everybody thought Jimmy was just a little bad and wild. But sometimes, oh my goodness, it's the opposite. It's the sweet-seeming boy who's successful—with good grades—maybe overly good, the way you were with your books and your chemistry set, so—

DR. MICHAELS   I'm well aware that perfectionism can be just as damaging.

MOM   "Perfectionism." You and your terms. Like words—even the biggest, fanciest ones can fix people. Like that little girl you seem to care so much about. That Frannie. (*looking up at Frannie, a girl of twelve who sits with her foster mom, Nora*) Why do you care about her so much, anyway? You know you're not supposed to have favorites. But you do, don't you.

DR. MICHAELS   So what?

MOM   She's just a little crazy person. Frannie, Frannie, Frannie. Like you're a little boy and she can be your friend. You can't go back, Robert. What's gone is gone.

DR. MICHAELS   I think I know that.

MOM   She's not your daughter. Not your blood.

DR. MICHAELS   No, she's just a kid born into a mess. Somehow. Some way. Just dropped into the world, because two idiots had sex. So that's her address. That's her street. That's her fate. How's that for terms? "Idiots." "Screwed-up parents." Ring any bells?

MOM   I don't know why you think it would.

DR. MICHAELS   C'mon.

MOM   No.

DR. MICHAELS   She's waiting. I can see Frannie in there inside herself hiding behind her eyes—vibrant and bright and waiting to trust.

MOM (*suddenly anguished*)   I'm dead. I'm wandering limbo—my soul between realms, lost among the nothings of everywhere and nowhere in the big big empty.

DR. MICHAELS   No you're not. You're in my head.

MOM   I'm lonely.

DR. MICHAELS   Bullshit. You're up to something.

MOM   I'm just trying to gnaw at you, that's all. I can't help it. Undermine your hopes, your confidence. That's all. I don't like seeing you this way.

DR. MICHAELS   What way?

MOM   Trying to save everybody. Like you're Jesus Christ or somebody.

DR. MICHAELS   I'm just me. I work. I think. If I were Jesus Christ it would be a different world.

MOM   Nobody saved me. Did they? Did they, Robert?

DR. MICHAELS   I'm going to bed. (*settling into one of the chairs*)

MOM   And sometimes it is the forlorn betrayed woman who you came home from school every afternoon to find on the couch drinking beer, the sad lonely woman who is the likely candidate— sometimes it is your mother who kills herself.

He toasts her as she goes.

And I am lonely.

DR. MICHAELS (*After watching her go, he turns to the audience*)   I have a confession. It's a fantasy I have. On the weekends, on Saturday nights, I belong to this group that gets together—has a beer or two and sings old songs. Songs going way back into the forties. Even the nineteen twenties. Really old ones. Every Saturday night we gather at someone's house, often not too far away, but other times I travel an hour or more. Once in a while it's here at my house. We sing and it calms me. Sooths me after the week. Now that's not the fantasy, of course, since I actually do it. The fantasy is that I like to imagine all my patients doing something similar sometimes—all singing together—I don't know where they are—some place—and they're singing and it's very, very peaceful. Or maybe they're alone. Or just with me. (*looking up at Jerome*) Jerome.

JEROME (*startled*)   What?

DR. MICHAELS   Do you ever sing? Would you like to sing?

JEROME   What?

DR. MICHAELS   Let's hear you.

JEROME   I don't do that, Dr. Michaels. I don't sing.

DR. MICHAELS   How about *On Moonlight Bay*?

JEROME   I don't sing, Dr. Michaels.

DR. MICHAELS   This isn't real. This is just pretend. I'm imagining it.

JEROME   Oh.

As this relaxes Jerome, he moves to Dr. Michaels who is near the piano.

DR. MICHAELS   Kind of dreaming. You know. Give it a little try. Let's try *On Moonlight Bay*. And do you know what? You can play the piano.

JEROME   What?

DR. MICHAELS   We should have a piano. You can play the piano and you play beautifully. It's not real, remember. It doesn't matter whether you know it or can do it. It's a simple tune, with lyrics I find exquisite.

Jerome is making his way to the piano.

MRS. GARLAND   I know it, Dr. Michaels.

JEROME (*settling onto the piano bench*)   He says I can play the piano, Mother.

DR. MICHAELS   Hello, Mrs. Garland.

Jerome starts to play the piano, and they sing.

MRS. GARLAND   Wonderful news. Wonderful.

DR. MICHAELS   "We were sailing along, on moonlight bay."

MRS. GARLAND   "We were sailing along, on moonlight bay."

DR. MICHAELS, MRS. GARLAND, & JEROME   We could hear the people singing. They seemed to say. You have stolen my heart, now don't go 'way. As we sing this old sweet song on moonlight bay. As we sing this old sweet song on moonlight bay.

EVANGELINE RYDER *along with* TIMOTHY, *who has a slightly disabled hand, have entered and are watching.*

TIMOTHY   Why aren't we singing, Evangeline?

EVANGELINE RYDER   Well, because, you see—that's happening in Dr. Michaels's imagination, and we aren't in it. At the moment.

TIMOTHY   Where are we?

EVANGELINE RYDER   Well, we're in my office . . . at the center where we're having a session and . . . (*Timothy sits in one of the chairs*) . . . you are very worried.

TIMOTHY   I am. I am very, very worried. They shouldn't be mean to me. I am a person with special needs. And they should know that and then they can think how I'm a person with special needs and be nice.

EVANGELINE RYDER   I don't think they intended to be mean to you, but—

TIMOTHY   BUT THEY ARE! THEY IGNORE ME AND I'M AN AGREEABLE PERSON! I'd like to widen my circle. Do I have a circle? Somebody said it's friends. Is that right?

EVANGELINE RYDER   Well, yes. Yes. In a way.

TIMOTHY   Okay. What way? Because I want friends. Not just the guys at the house. But friends everywhere. Because then I can have some "For old times sake" someday. You're not my friend. You're my therapist. And I want a girlfriend. Because I want to get married. I don't think I will have children though. My mom and dad like my brother's kids, but they're rude and messy. So no kids for me. That's what I think. What do you think?

EVANGELINE RYDER   Is that what you've decided?

TIMOTHY   After due consideration that's what I decided. Are you proud of me?

EVANGELINE RYDER   I'm always proud of you. You're my hero.

TIMOTHY   Okay. What does that mean? Oh, oh. I forgot. Where's my circle, Evangeline? Where is it?

EVANGELINE RYDER   We can talk about that in a minute, Timothy, but I think it's important that we first do some work to help you come to a better understanding of how to meet and talk to people without scaring them.

TIMOTHY   NO!

EVANGELINE RYDER   I know you don't want to talk about the trouble at the McDonalds, but you need to understand what happened and how to avoid making the same mistakes again.

TIMOTHY   DON'T SAY I MADE MISTAKES. SHE WAS THERE AND I WAS THERE and I wanted to be agreeable. We were both agreeable people. One with disabilities—that would be me—and one without.

EVANGELINE RYDER   But she got scared.

TIMOTHY I WASN'T BEING SCARY—I WAS BEING AGREEABLE. He was mean. He was very mean.

EVANGELINE RYDER Well, he was her husband, so he wanted to protect her.

TIMOTHY Am I king of the world?

EVANGELINE RYDER Why do you ask?

TIMOTHY He said that. That man. "You really think you're king of the world, don't you buddy." What is that?

EVANGELINE RYDER Well, it's when somebody is bossy, and they think they're everybody's boss.

TIMOTHY Can I be king of the world?

EVANGELINE RYDER No. No one can, Timothy. No one anywhere.

TIMOTHY But why did he say it then? He must have had his facts upside down.

EVANGELINE RYDER He was angry and worried. That's why he said he was calling the police.

TIMOTHY He was going to call 911, and he was yelling.

EVANGELINE RYDER Thank goodness you told him to call the house instead and gave him the card with the house number so the staff could hurry over and explain. We don't want anyone ever calling 911.

TIMOTHY No we don't.

EVANGELINE RYDER Because it might be a mean policeman who comes—or two mean policemen. So I think let's talk about why the trouble happened.

TIMOTHY I just said "Hello."

EVANGELINE RYDER But you followed that woman from one table to the next and you wouldn't stop saying hello. And her husband came then—

TIMOTHY   He was in the bathroom.

EVANGELINE RYDER   This is why we have to do your social skills training. It will help you learn the right way to say "hello" to people who don't know you, so you can be responsible and—

TIMOTHY (*indignant, fists clenched*)   I AM RESPONSIBLE!

EVANGELINE RYDER   I know you are.

TIMOTHY   I AM VERY RESPONSIBLE! I take my medicine every morning and night and I do it so the nurse can watch me every step of the way. And I take care of Otto.

EVANGELINE RYDER   Yes you do. Otto is a very lucky hamster.

TIMOTHY   He's just a poor helpless hamster who would die if I didn't take care of him. So he's lucky, because I do take care of him. And he smiles sometimes when he's running on his treadmill, like he's going somewhere, I don't tell him he's not. But I laugh. He's funny. So I'm lucky too. We're both lucky.

EVANGELINE RYDER   I couldn't agree more. But at the McDonalds—even when the woman got up and walked to the bathroom, you followed her.

TIMOTHY   And he came out of the other bathroom and I said "Hello," and he called me king of the world, even though there isn't one.

EVANGELINE RYDER   And then he and his wife walked out to their car in the parking lot, and you followed them.

TIMOTHY   I WANTED TO SAY "GOODBYE." "Hello" and "Goodbye."

EVANGELINE RYDER   Of course you did. And your social skills training can help you so you get off on the right foot. We need to practice. Right now. I want you to watch me. I'll do it—then you—(*as he turns away*) Timothy, watch me. C'mon now. (*as he looks back*) If we didn't know each other, and I wanted to say "hello," to you, I would look at you and say, "hello." And then look away. (*demonstrating*) You can't stare at people after you say "hello." It makes them nervous. Especially if they're a woman and you're a man. So look away and count slowly to six. If they say "hello" back, then you might say—if you are at McDonalds—you might say, "These are good french fries." But that's all. If they don't answer, you cannot keep saying hello.

TIMOTHY   Maybe they don't hear me.

EVANGELINE RYDER   You talk very clearly and loudly, Timothy. Now show me how you will say "hello."

TIMOTHY (*turning to her*)   Hello. (*staring at her*)

EVANGELINE RYDER   Now look away.

He looks away, almost violently.

Good job, Timothy. Good job. Now count to six like we—

TIMOTHY   ONE! TWO!

EVANGELINE RYDER   No, Timothy. Silently in your head.

They wait as he counts to about four and stops.

TIMOTHY   What's my circle again and how do I widen it?

EVANGELINE RYDER   Well, yes, it's friends, like you thought. A circle of friends.

TIMOTHY   What would it be? It would be what?

EVANGELINE RYDER   Well, it would be if you were there in your chair and your friends were all in a circle around you. There and there . . . . (*As Timothy turns, following the circle as she places his imagined friends*) . . . and there and there . . . and there, too. In a circle around you.

She turns and goes. Timothy hurries after her. Frannie stands up and bounds down from her area, as Dr. Michaels enters.

FRANNIE I'm one two three four five six seven eight nine ten eleven twelve years old.

Frannie ends up standing on top of the piano/desk. Dr. Michaels looks up at her. Nora has moved to one of the waiting room chairs.

DR. MICHAELS Frannie, come down off my desk, all right? You know that's not allowed.

FRANNIE (*not budging*) What are years?

DR. MICHAELS Well . . . years? What do you think they are?

FRANNIE I know what deers are, and beers and tears. Tell me what you think. I don't know.

DR. MICHAELS Come down now and let's sit in the chairs and talk about it.

FRANNIE No.

But she takes his offered hand and comes down, hopping to the floor.

I ask you and you ask me is stupid.

DR. MICHAELS What do you mean?

FRANNIE (*sitting in one of the chairs*) I ask you "what are years," and you ask me "what are years." That's stupid. Doesn't anybody know?

DR. MICHAELS Well, years are a measurement of time, which people—

FRANNIE What's time? People say "what time is it? What time is it?"

DR. MICHAELS Yes, they do. Say if you're going to school, and you don't want to be late, then—

FRANNIE How tall are you? You're very very tall. If I stand next to you I'm tiny. (*she moves close to him*) You could be a giant.

DR. MICHAELS Do you think I'm that tall? I'm not really so—

FRANNIE Sometimes I have storms. Big big big storms inside me. It's thunder and lightning inside me.

DR. MICHAELS   I know. I was thinking how that must be very hard, Frannie, and scary. Do you know what makes the storms happen?

FRANNIE   What?

DR. MICHAELS   I mean, are there certain things you think about, or certain things that happen and then—

FRANNIE   The sky makes storms you idiot, And wind, this big black wind and there's rain and howling and god maybe is pissed off, or mad cause he's dying and "oh god, oh god," he says, "I'm dying," and black skies and no moon and all inside me. And I'm really little. I'm not very big. And they just go on and on, these big booming storms, and me and the storm are both—(*she screams, kind of wild eyed, breathless and scared*) You looked scared. Did I scare you? Storms are scary. So look out. I try to look out. Do you have any broken glass or nails or pins, or a paper clip, because you can straighten it out and just stick yourself and the storm goes away.

DR. MICHAELS   But that hurts, doesn't it.

FRANNIE   Why don't you know what years are? Are you stupid?

DR. MICHAELS   I do know.

FRANNIE   Then why don't you tell me. Go get a pin and I'll show you. You just stick it and it's like a big balloon goes hisssss and all the air goes out and the balloon feels empty and I'm a big balloon going hisssssss and getting— Go hisssssss. Like that.

DR. MICHAELS   Me?

FRANNIE   Why not? Are you scared?

DR. MICHAELS   No.

FRANNIE   Don't you like me? It's a favor. I want a favor.

DR. MICHAELS   Of course I like you.

FRANNIE   Then go hisssss. Tell me what years are, damnit. Tell me what time is, damnit, damnit. You're stupid. I want to see my mommy. My real mommy—not that stupid Nora, but Trish Alice

128

Metzinger, my real mommy. My birth mommy who born me into the world. Go hisssss you stupid Doctor.

DR. MICHAELS All right. But only as a favor. Hiissssssss.

Frannie seems disgusted with him.

FRANNIE That wasn't very realistic at all.

DR. MICHAELS Frannie.

FRANNIE Are you mad at me?

DR. MICHAELS No. I just—I think I want to talk to Nora for a minute. Is that all right?

FRANNIE I don't care. She's stupid you know. So you two should get along. You're both stupid. That's what Trish says. You're birds of a feather—Dr. Busybody and Mzzzz Goodie Two-shoes. (*as he moves to go*) Can I have a book to read?

DR. MICHAELS That's a good idea. I have several there. On top of the desk. (*gesturing to a stack of children's books on the desk*) You can pick whichever one you want.

As Frannie looks at the books, Dr. Michaels goes into the waiting room, where Nora rises.

NORA You see? Do you see? I told you.

DR. MICHAELS It's worse, I agree, but not so bad. She's just a little—

NORA What are you talking about? It's horrible.

DR. MICHAELS She's hyper and a little manic, but—

NORA As far as I'm concerned, this is as ever. As ever! I can't think straight, if I'm not making any sense, you'll have to fill in the blanks. I'm so tired. I can't take much more.

DR. MICHAELS Nora, I know how hard it is, but you've got to hang in.

NORA I'm trying.

DR. MICHAELS We'll figure it out. We'll—

NORA I wish I believed that.

DR. MICHAELS Don't start reconsidering whether or not you will adopt Frannie. Please. She'll get better.

NORA Do you have a crystal ball in these matters? I'm sorry. But do you?

DR. MICHAELS Something must trigger her manic states—these "fits" as you call them. Are you aware of any kind of pattern?

NORA There are times when I think there's improvement, and then . . . I don't know.

DR. MICHAELS There must be something.

NORA Oh, what the hell are we hemming and hawing about? It's her visits with her birth mother and we both know it. She goes over there and—because she's crazy, you know—Trish Metzinger is crazy—and Frannie sees her and comes back crazy.

DR. MICHAELS They have to stop then.

NORA I've been saying that for months. I've been begging.

DR. MICHAELS The visits have to stop. I've been talking to Protective Services but I'll push harder.

NORA And ask them to make sense will you? That would be a really big, really useful first step. Half the time I can't tell what Protective Services is saying. Not even whether they think I can still adopt Frannie or not.

DR. MICHAELS I assure you. You can. You can adopt Frannie. It's what everybody wants. The state terminated parental rights on Frannie's older brother on grounds of parental neglect and sexual abuse, so this is an open and shut case.

NORA   And yet it isn't, is it? In any real way, because it just drags on and on. These fits—you haven't really seen a bad one—I can't comfort her. It's like she doesn't even see me or hear me. I have to fight her to make her stop. It's overwhelming. I can't think. Let me think.

Struggling to think, Nora turns away.

Meanwhile, Frannie, seated in a chair and trying to read the book, has been increasingly restless, twisting in her chair, as if to escape fire. And Mom has entered and moved close. Now Mom leans in, whispering in Frannie's ear.

MOM   Go listen at the door, little crazy person. They're out there talking about you. That lying stupid giant and that stupid idiotic Nora. They're deciding what's going to happen to you. Don't you just hate her. She's so pitiful and ignorant, the two of them talking about you as if you don't exist.

Frannie crosses toward Nora and Dr. Michaels and stands, as if eavesdropping at a door. Mom moves closer.

That's right, you little moron. Put your ear to the door. But sneakily, so you can hear them plotting out your life without you—deciding what they want to do to you next.

NORA   They're all drug addicts—her and whatever random idiot she's got in her bed on any particular day. It's common knowledge.

DR. MICHAELS   She came for counseling, and I thought we were making progress, but then she stopped.

NORA   Did she come alone, or was she with one of her—(*making air quotes*) "Boyfriends?"

DR. MICHAELS   I can't say, Nora. You know that.

NORA   Oh, sure, let's be discrete about her. Not that it matters which one of her assorted goons she dragged in here. They're all like her pets, except the one's who get sick of it and smacks her around. (*laughing*) Why am I laughing? Because she stopped counseling. Of course she stopped counseling. Not the drugs. Stop the drugs? Are you kidding? I don't know what happens to Frannie when she's over there but I'm worried it's awful. I keep thinking how she tried to get this boy at school involved in something sexual—some kind of sexual game.

DR. MICHAELS It's disturbing. I know.

NORA Right. You know, I know, we all know. Yesterday she beat up another child at school. She can't keep bouncing back and forth.

Frannie charges into the waiting room, where Nora grabs her.

FRANNIE When the storm stops, I stop.

NORA She's . . . scaring me, Dr. Michaels.

DR. MICHAELS Have you been listening, Frannie?

FRANNIE Anybody with a storm inside them would do the same things and don't think they wouldn't. Because you would. Just try having a storm inside you.

DR. MICHAELS Have you been listening?

FRANNIE No. To what?

DENISE, *the secretary, enters the door from the reception area, carrying folders of paperwork.*

DENISE Bob, do you have a minute?

DR. MICHAELS Not just now.

DENISE Bob, please, you really have to give me a minute. I don't need long.

DR. MICHAELS Not this second. What are you doing? You can't burst in on a session like this, Denise and you know it.

DENISE You're in the waiting room, Bob. (*to Nora*) And I'm sorry, Ms. Meyers, but the session is over. Your session has been over for ten minutes.

NORA Oh. I'm sorry. I'm really sorry. (*taking Frannie by the hand*) I'll go. We'll go. Come, Frannie. We have to go.

Rushing, Nora and Frannie go.

DENISE You really have to stop avoiding all this.

DR. MICHAELS All of what, Denise?

DENISE The cost/loss aspects of any number of cases that are getting away from us. And Frannie Bascome is a prime example. Her case is a disaster since Colossal Care took over as benefits manager and—

DR. MICHAELS They don't handle Frannie. She's under Everyday Health.

DENISE It's six months since Colossal Care took over. We both know you hate all this paperwork, but I need you to focus. The before and after statistics on the Frannie Bascome case illustrate a disarming trend.

DR. MICHAELS Which is what?

DENISE We're not getting paid. That's the trend. Before C.C.I. became Benefits manager, we saw Frannie twenty-nine times over a ten month period and we were reimbursed thirty-five dollars and seventy-five cents per session. Given the fact that each of those sessions cost us one hundred dollars to provide that's a loss of sixty-four dollars per session. Which is a total loss of eighteen hundred and fifty-six dollars on one case over a—

DR. MICHAELS Wait. Wait, wait. Why are we talking about before? If Everyday Health is no longer —

DENISE Because "after" gets worse. Colossal Care is reimbursing us more per session, but they refused to approve any repayment for ten sessions. So that's ten sessions for which we received nothing. Not a dime.

DR. MICHAELS Get her case manager on the phone. I've got ten minutes right now.

DENISE Are you kidding me? You're asking for a miracle. Getting them on the phone is a full time job. (*handing him a document*) I've summarized the problem which stems mainly from their guidelines that you'd think Moses brought down from the mount—and when I do actually get them, then you're in session or busy or—

DR. MICHAELS Just get them. I'll talk.

Annoyed, Denise marches off.

DENISE You don't know what you're asking.

DR. MICHAELS Denise, I'm not blaming you.

As Denise goes without having looked back, Mom has drifted in.

MOM Robert, Robert, Robert. Don't lie. You are too blaming her. You certainly are. I warned you about that little girl—about getting too involved. And now you're losing perspective. Acting like everything is Denise's fault—the whole system—when you know you hate all this paperwork, as if you're somehow above it. You and Frannie. Off in the clouds somehow.

DR. MICHAELS You have got to shut up!

He exits, as a phone starts to ring and Denise enters, aswering the phone.

SWITCHBOARD OPERATOR Hello. Northwood Mental Health Center.

Lights up on Teresa and Barnard, both in their seventies.

TERESA Can I talk to someone there?

SWITCHBOARD OPERATOR This is the switchboard. Do you need a counselor? There's several people—

TERESA My husband won't get out of bed.

SWITCHBOARD OPERATOR Perhaps you'd like to make an appointment.

TERESA No, no. Do you make house calls?

SWITCHBOARD OPERATOR What do you mean, he won't get out of bed? Do you mean he won't go to work, or he's not feeling well or—

TERESA No, no, we're retired. He gets up to go to the bathroom and that's all, and it's been weeks. I'm talking about weeks. (*turning to her husband*) Get up goddamnit. Right now. Get up.

BARNARD I see no reason to get up.

SWITCHBOARD OPERATOR It's been weeks, you said? How many weeks?

TERESA (*to husband*) How long do you think I can keep doing this and bearing the whole load? I'm going batty with this way you're acting! I'm going batty.

BARNARD I just can't right now. That's all.

TERESA He says he can't get up right now.

SWITCHBOARD OPERATOR Is he depressed?

TERESA I don't know if he is, but I sure am.

BARNARD What? You are what?

TERESA Depressed.

BARNARD No, I'm not.

TERESA You are. Of course you are.

BARNARD No. I feel empty.

TERESA He says he's not depressed, he feels empty.

SWITCHBOARD OPERATOR I'm sorry, what?

TERESA He feels empty.

BARNARD Empty. Seventy goddamn years old and I feel empty.

SWITCHBOARD OPERATOR I'm going to get someone—I'm going to see who's available to talk to you. ·

TERESA   No, no, I'm asking do you make house calls?

SWITCHBOARD OPERATOR   Hold on please. Did you tell me your name?

TERESA   I'm Teresa Gilchrist.

SWITCHBOARD OPERATOR   All right, Mrs. Gilchrist. And your husband is—?

BARNARD (*loudly, as he rises to enter the main area*)   Barnard! I'm Barnard. I was just—I was just—the dog had vomited on the basement stairs and I was going to have to clean it up. (*addressing the audience, he wanders about*) But I wanted to drink this morning drink I take of vitamins, because I'd been feeling a lot of fatigue, lately, a lot of it, and so I made my drink and I was drinking it, and then I had to go to the bathroom and on my way back from the bathroom, I had the drink in my right hand and I was doing my best to get back to where I started. I don't know what I was thinking about—I think—that it was my—when I— There's a lot behind me you know, a lot behind a person when he gets to my age, and not much in front of you, so it's all lopsided, this life that's bulging out behind you, and so I could have been thinking about a lot a things, and I think—I think—No, no. I don't remember. That's the truth. I don't really remember what I was thinking about, I want to, and I want to think I do, and claim I do, but I don't. I have no idea. But I had the drink in my hand and I was walking, when my other hand, my left hand—the drink was in my right hand and my godforsaken left hand came up for no reason I can remember and hit the drink. My left hand smacked into the drink almost knocking it out of my right hand. It had some purpose—my left hand, I remember this vague sense of purpose—that it was going to do something, which sure as hell was not to hit the drink, but something else, and it was on it's way to do that, ostensibly. But what it did instead was slam-crash into the edge of the glass, tilting it almost out of my fingers and pouring about half of what was in the glass down on our beautiful Persian rug. This big gigantic yellow splatter. I looked at it and stood there looking because cleaning it up seemed like this big job, this big damn task so big it would take the rest of what was left of my life. But I figured I better get started and I went into the kitchen to get some rags or something, sponges to wipe the rug, and as I was in the kitchen, the phone rang and I answered, hoping it was—I don't know who, but hoping something because I picked it up with this energy, this expectation, and what it was was this phone company trying to get my business back. We'd been with this particular phone company for a while, but we had recently switched to a different phone company that had called soliciting us, and now the company we had abandoned wanted us back. I said, "No," we were happy with our new phone company, but this woman on the other end insisted on running her whole spiel at me, about everything they would "Give me," and it made me sad to hear her because I knew she was this complete stranger and I knew she just wanted my money. She wanted her money, her salary, and to get that she had to try and get my money for her company so they would give her her money. Well, I sat there listening, because I knew she was just some poor desperate woman doing her desperate stupid job and I felt, for just this particular second, I felt sad for everybody on earth, but particularly her and me, and I told her that I had to get off the line a couple of times, but she didn't give up, so I sat there wishing I could be rude, worried about being rude, why couldn't I be rude, and then finally it was over. She said she'd sign me up and I said, "No. No, don't sign me up. I have to go." I hung up and looked down at the rags and sponge in my hand and I had no idea what they were for until I remembered the dog vomit on the stairs and went and got to cleaning it up when my wife screamed—she screamed about something awful, something hideous on the rug. Which was of course the spilled drink. I said it was just the spilled drink. "What spilled drink?" She wanted to know. It was a natural enough question but it seemed unnecessary. What did it matter, "What spilled drink?" Considering everything going on in the world at that moment, what did it matter? I didn't answer; couldn't answer really, my tongue was so thick and numb, I couldn't move it. I went and knelt down on the Persian rug and looked at all the dead Persians depicted on horses or in wagons or walking along the tapestry, tiptoeing over the threads with big pieces of pottery in their arms. I cleaned the spilled drink up and my wife helped and it didn't take long, maybe a few minutes, and then she smiled and rushed out to the car to drive away to have coffee with her friend, Alice. (*somewhat wistfully*) And I watched her go, and then I went to bed.

He sits in one of the chairs as Evangeline Ryder enters to settle in the other chair.

EVANGELINE RYDER   And you stayed in bed.

BARNARD   So far. Except for letting my wife haul me in here to see you.

EVANGELINE RYDER   And it all started two weeks ago?

BARNARD   That's what she says.

EVANGELINE RYDER   And this—is this the first time any such thing has—

BARNARD   Like this? Happened to me?

EVANGELINE RYDER   Yes. That it's happened.

BARNARD   No, no, no. Oh, no.

EVANGELINE RYDER   I see.

BARNARD   When I was in my mid-twenties which—believe it or not, I once was. It happened.

EVANGELINE RYDER   I see. And what brought it on?

BARNARD   Well, I'm the wrong person to ask about that. I have no idea what brought it on. I mean, there were the usual things, like this girl I thought I loved, and she jilted me. Things like that. The usual things. But ending up in bed, well, that was a pretty unusual solution. "Whata bum," everybody said. She had this uncle to whom she was devoted, an uncle who had in fact raised her and he got killed in an accident in this factory where he worked in steel—this foundry, and something awful happened to him. This machine he worked with every day—he made a mistake or someone else made a mistake, and it fell on him—or maybe he got caught in it—I can't remember actually, but he was crushed to death. He was a big man—like my dad. They were big men with big thick hands—worker hands. He was a rough customer—but not rough enough for that machine. Then Abigail just turned her back on me. It didn't make any sense why what happened would cause her to give me the cold shoulder, but she did, I was like this yowling cat so she threw her shoe at me and somebody else dumped cold water on me, and she was done with me, didn't even want to be friends, and I was sad for a long time. I was sad for a whole year at least.

EVANGELINE RYDER   And you lay in bed—all that time?

BARNARD   There was a week or two is all. I was ashamed, you know, so I got up.

EVANGELINE RYDER   And now?

BARNARD   Now? Well, who gives a goddamn?!

EVANGELINE RYDER   And you're seventy-five, is that right?

BARNARD   So they tell me. And then maybe twenty years later it almost happened again. I was married now with kids and a successful business and I started thinking one day of the way that machine had turned suddenly from an implement of labor into a killing thing crushing Abigail's uncle. I got this feeling I was headed back to bed. But I got this other feeling that there was maybe something I could learn to stop it, and so I started off reading. Almost sneaky, like it was a crime. I was reading all these books like *I and Thou* by Martin Buber. And this other one he wrote. Ever hear of him?

EVANGELINE RYDER   Yes, I certainly have.

BARNARD   And *The Tao of Physics*. I read that. And *The Dancing Wu Li Masters*. I bet you never heard of them. My daughter had them, even though they were from this era supposed to give you answers almost before she was born. I read *The Cloud of Unknowing* and some full-fledged physics books, and *Meister Echart, the Essential Sermons*.

No one knew what I was doing. I didn't know what I was doing, but what I was doing was I was looking for meaning. For a meaning to life beyond what was normally taken to be enough meaning, something else, something more, and I was hoping to find it, and I kept reading and reading but I never did find it.

EVANGELINE RYDER You didn't.

BARNARD No. Have you?

EVANGELINE RYDER Have I what? Oh. Well, no, I guess. Not really.

BARNARD Have you looked?

EVANGELINE RYDER Well, not in the way you did.

BARNARD I don't think I looked in any particular way. I just looked.

EVANGELINE RYDER Well, I suppose then—I mean, you said—"more than is normally taken for enough meaning," or some such phrase, and on that basis, if that's the criteria, I suppose I haven't.

BARNARD Let me give you a word of advice, if you don't mind. Don't bother.

EVANGELINE RYDER The way you put it is interesting, though. Would you be willing to come in again, Barnard, and talk about this some more with me?

BARNARD You think it's interesting, huh?

EVANGELINE RYDER I'll set up a time.

BARNARD Sure. What the hell, I've already wasted most of my life—wouldn't want to change now. (*rising and starting to go, he stops and looks back*) And I read *The Drama of the Gifted Child* back then, too, and that one took the cake—that was the saddest of them all, when I read about the false self. Because I felt I was reading about a hero, maybe the greatest, bravest hero ever is what I felt, because he didn't hardly exist—had nothing inside, nothing to hang onto, or refer to, but went forth anyway, just you know, desperately hoping to live. That one really got me.

EVANGELINE RYDER   Is next Monday—at say, 3:15 good for you?

BARNARD   Sure. I guess you're some kind of a glutton for punishment.

EVANGELINE RYDER   I guess. (*rising to go*) Well, to be continued.

As Evangeline goes off Barnard returns to his area, and we enter a SURREAL space of night and sound, where Dr. Michaels enters, turning, searching.

DR. MICHAELS   Frannie? Frannie, I can't sleep.

Frannie comes down from her area.

FRANNIE   Dr. Michaels? Dr. Michaels. I can't sleep.

Walking backwards as they search, they bump into each other.

DR. MICHAELS   There you are.

FRANNIE   Where?

DR. MICHAELS   In my imagination.

FRANNIE   Oh. Okay.

DR. MICHAELS   You have so much to figure out. Your young life and long future. While I can look back and see myself small like you.

FRANNIE   Can you look back and see me?

Mom stirs in her elevated area and they look up to see her watching them.

MOM   I just want to listen.

DR. MICHAELS   I know how storms are big and scary when you're little because I had them, too. But there's a song I used to sing to banish them, and maybe you can sing it, too, and banish yours. Then you wouldn't have to stick or cut yourself.

FRANNIE   What is it? (*surprised*) Oh, wait! I know it. Even though it's way way olden. It's too olden for me to have ever heard it and yet I know it, and I love it. And it goes like this: (*Singing*) "Glow little glow-worm, glimmer, glimmer. Shine little glow-worm, shimmer,

141

shimmer. Lead us lest we too far wander. Love's sweet voice is calling yonder. Shine little glow-worm, glimmer, glimmer. Hey there, don't get dimmer, dim—"

NORA   Frannie, what are you doing?

As Nora walks toward them.

FRANNIE   I'm in Dr. Michaels imagination and singing and it's nice.

NORA   Am I there, too?

FRANNIE   Maybe. My foot hurts.

NORA   Did something happen to it?

FRANNIE   It's dark, too very dark. I want to go back to bed.

NORA   Honey, it's night. That's all.

FRANNIE   There's clouds.

NORA   Are you teasing? The sky is bright and clear tonight. Look out the window at the stars. I don't see any clouds.

FRANNIE   They're hiding. They're over behind the wind. Because they're hiding on the bottom side of the world. Thunder's coming.

NORA   I don't hear anything.

FRANNIE   Big and black clouds all full of noise and wind and rain and snow and all these big wild horses dragging it closer. Big thunder's coming.

NORA   I really don't hear it.

FRANNIE   Oh, it's there. Shhhhhh. (*whispering*) Listen.

As Frannie, Nora and Dr. Michaels listen, Jerome stirs.

JEROME   Dr. Michaels?

DR. MICHAELS   Shhhh.

JEROME   What? Excuse me?

DR. MICHAELS   Not now. I'm trying to hear Frannie's thunder. The thunder inside her—I need to hear it and understand it, because then I—

JEROME   But I'm waiting, Dr. Michaels. I've been waiting and waiting.

DR. MICHAELS   What? (*realizing: seeing Jerome*) Oh. Jerome.

Jerome moves toward Dr. Michaels and the chairs.

JEROME   It's not easy, you know. Waiting.

DR. MICHAELS   I'm sorry. Of course. You're right.

JEROME   Or coping. Or trying to make progress. All my boxes. I get very upset when they move. Or people move them. Some people think—just throw it all out. Just throw it all out. My mom, she just picks things up sometimes and moves them. She has no respect for my things. I get so mad, I'd like to just—I really want to just— (*stopping, he stands there*)

DR. MICHAELS   I thought she was coming to session today.

JEROME   She is, but she had an errand to run first. (*starting to sit, he stands up*) Should we wait for her?

DR. MICHAELS   No. We can start. Tell me more about the progress you mentioned.

JEROME (*sitting*)   It's with the boxes of magazines like you and I talked about, so I can finally move into my new apartment. The magazines and all the articles I plan to read some day but haven't had time yet. Well, I organized them into categories; like a *Current Events* category; and another is *Literary;* and there's *Sports*. And then there's *Miscellaneous*. That was a big one.

DR. MICHAELS   Terrific, Jerome. Well done. So are you ready to move then?

JEROME   Almost. Yes. Almost ready. I didn't say I completed everything. Don't misunderstand. Because there are all these other boxes, and piles of things and stuff which are more or less untouched and so they're more or less completely unorganized.

As Mrs. Garland enters through the reception area door. Late forties, she wears a neck support collar and she is wounded by everything.

MRS. GARLAND That's right. And what they are Dr. Michaels—all those unorganized ones—is a tragic mess.

JEROME A large number—a very large number of the boxes which were unorganized are now organized, Mom. And you know it.

MRS. GARLAND And the category for everything left "unorganized"—if you want to know—that category would be . . . ugly trash. (*so wounded again*)

JEROME You don't understand anything.

MRS. GARLAND So what category would you say they are? I'm desperate to know.

JEROME I don't know, Mother. I have no idea.

MRS. GARLAND Then how can you organize them by category? See, these are the kinds of plans he makes! It just breaks my heart.

JEROME I don't know what you're talking about.

MRS. GARLAND Stop picking at your skin. (*grabbing at his arm*) Keep that up for one more second and your arm is going to be bleeding right in front of us.

JEROME I didn't even know I was doing it.

MRS. GARLAND (*begging*) Dr. Michaels, can't you make him stop picking at his skin? It's so unhealthy and unattractive.

JEROME (*rising, walking*) Don't push me. Everybody has got to stop pushing me. I'm warning you.

MRS. GARLAND Am I pushing him, Dr. Michaels? Now he's threatening me. (*sitting in the chair Jerome left*)

DR. MICHAELS Jerome, in all the time we've been seeing each other, I think you —

JEROME It's four months and twenty-two days. That's how long.

DR. MICHAELS Yes. That sounds about right. And I was going to say that at least once in every session you've said how eager you are to move.

JEROME I am. And as soon as I get these other categories of boxes to straightened out, I will, believe me.

MRS. GARLAND What's in them? Help me to understand, Jerome.

JEROME Well, there's mainly things that I find particularly interesting, in as far as I think they will come in handy.

DR. MICHAELS Jerome.

MRS. GARLAND Handy for what? For what will these things you're filling you're room with come in handy?

JEROME I don't even know what they are, half of them.

MRS. GARLAND It's all so hopeless and sad and terrible and awful. The mess, the mess.

JEROME We just don't value the same things, Mother!

DR. MICHAELS Jerome!

JEROME What?

DR. MICHAELS Last week, you decided that the main obstacle keeping you from moving was the fact that your boxes were so disorganized. But you thought that if you worked—if you moved them to the new apartment in stages, you could handle it. You're not moving that far, after all. It's only down into the basement.

JEROME It's not the basement.

MRS. GARLAND Dr. Michaels, no, no, it's a basement apartment.

JEROME And I'm not so sure I really, fully, completely decided.

MRS. GARLAND He never decides anything completely. I could just start bawling.

JEROME But I was almost ready—I was right on the verge, right on the edge.

DR. MICHAELS Then why didn't you?

MRS. GARLAND I had a car crash. What's that got to do with it?

JEROME She hit a tree.

MRS. GARLAND There was black ice, Dr. Michaels, but I didn't see it.

JEROME And then part of the tree—some of the big branches— one in particular of these very big branches fell down on top of the roof of the car.

MRS. GARLAND Scared me to death.

DR. MICHAELS And so, Jerome? Because your mother had a car crash, you couldn't move.

MRS. GARLAND That's why I have my whiplash collar on, Dr. Michaels.

DR. MICHAELS I'm sorry to hear that.

JEROME I had to help her. She was pretty banged up.

DR. MICHAELS Jerome. I want to point something out, but I want to be accurate. How long has it been that you've been trying to move into the basement?

JEROME It's not the basement.

MRS. GARLAND Dr. Michaels, it's so disappointing that you keep saying that. It's a very nice apartment. It's just in the basement.

DR. MICHAELS I'm sure it is. But you've been trying to move down those two flights of stairs from the upstairs bedroom where you currently live for how long, Jerome?

MRS. GARLAND It hasn't been all that long, I don't think, has it, Jerome?

JEROME It's been three years.

DR. MICHAELS So for three years something keeps stopping you.

JEROME I guess.

DR. MICHAELS Something gets in the way.

JEROME (*eager to learn*) What?

DR. MICHAELS That's what I'm asking you, Jerome.

MRS. GARLAND The boxes get in the way, I'll tell you that, and it just breaks my heart.

JEROME I can't just throw them out. Because I mean, there's projects of value in them that I want a chance to finish.

MRS. GARLAND You'll never finish them. Never. Just like you'll never move.

JEROME I will, too, finish them. And I will, too, move. You tell her, Dr. Michaels. You tell her I will too move.

Pleading, Jerome steps toward Dr. Michaels. The lights take a slight surreal shift.

DR. MICHAELS Wait, wait. Let's sing. I want the three of us to sing a beautiful old tune.

JEROME What?

Dr. Michaels turns to the audience, as Jerome and Mrs. Garland freeze.

DR. MICHAELS I didn't actually do that. But there are times during certain sessions, when I think about it—actually asking them to sing. In reality. Right in our chairs. But then I see it's not a good idea.

A loud sound, a CRASH, and in a burst of light, Nora and Frannie move toward Dr. Michaels.

NORA We're coming over. I don't care! This second! I walked into her room thinking we might go out for ice cream, and there was blood all over the sheets. It was this nightmare thing right in front of me. She was stabbing her arm with a paper clip—like it was a little knife, and I don't even know where she got it. I wrapped a T-shirt around her arm and ran out to get towels and peroxide—I heard this crash, because she'd broken a lamp so she could use the pieces to cut her arm. It's the middle of the afternoon—a beautiful day and I was thinking about ice cream.

Frannie, her forearms wrapped in gauze, has settled onto one of the chairs, bowed over, weakly, her voice small when she speaks.

DR. MICHAELS Frannie.

He approaches gently, while Nora stands on the opposite side of the chair, watching.

FRANNIE What?

DR. MICHAELS What happened?

FRANNIE When?

DR. MICHAELS You must have been very upset?

FRANNIE When?

DR. MICHAELS When you cut yourself this way—when you broke that lamp and started to cut yourself—

FRANNIE I didn't break it. It broke itself.

DR. MICHAELS What?

NORA She doesn't remember. She says.

FRANNIE I didn't do it.

DR. MICHAELS (*indicating the bandages*) Does she need to have this looked at? Can I see, Frannie?

NORA She has to know what happened, doesn't she?

148

FRANNIE I remember not breaking it is what I remember. It broke itself, I think.

DR. MICHAELS Why would it do that?

FRANNIE I don't know. Ask it.

DR. MICHAELS Ask the lamp?

FRANNIE Yes. See what it says.

DR. MICHAELS But it's a lamp. It can't talk, can it?

FRANNIE Maybe.

DR. MICHAELS Maybe it can talk?

FRANNIE Maybe.

DR. MICHAELS What would it say if it could talk?

FRANNIE It would say maybe it broke itself and I was sleeping.

NORA And the other night, she threw a chair through the window.

FRANNIE Did not!

NORA Well, it didn't jump.

FRANNIE It could have!

Nora moves past Frannie in order to consult privately with Dr. Michaels.

NORA It's because she told Protective Services that she wanted to stay with me and not go back to her birth mother. Everything went bonkers almost the second she said it. Why do they make her decide? They should decide. We should decide. And she's still seeing Trish, even after saying she doesn't want to live with her. After she's picked me. They're still making her visit. It's nuts.

DR. MICHAELS The court-appointed psychiatrist recommended that parental rights be terminated, and so they will be—

NORA Nine months ago! But Protective Services hasn't done it— and so, of course, in this one area Trish is determined to go by the letter of the law, and something awful is happening to Frannie when she goes there. I know it.

Denise hurries in from the reception area.

DENISE Bob, I've got C.C.I. on line six, can you take it? I actually got them. And please don't say "Not now!"

DR. MICHAELS Nora, when is Frannie's next session? Is it scheduled?

NORA Are you saying I should leave? I don't want to leave. Can't I stay and have a session when you're off the call?

DR. MICHAELS You know C.C.I. won't allow that.

NORA Not even now? When things are like this?

DR. MICHAELS Come back first thing in the morning—arrange it with Denise—I'll make it happen—and I'll recommend to Frannie's psychiatrist that we change her medication.

The C.C.I. Rep. MARCY walks on, pacing.

MARCY Hello! Hello! This is C.C.I. I'm waiting. I can't stay on hold forever. I'm counting down from ten. (*which she does, softly*)

NORA I'm afraid to be alone with her.

DR. MICHAELS I'm sorry, Nora, but I have to take this call.

As Frannie and Nora scurry away, Dr. Michaels addresses Marcy on the phone call.

Listen, this has to get straightened out.

MARCY To whom am I speaking?

Dr. Michaels and Marcy pace and talk.

DR. MICHAELS Dr. Michaels. This is Dr. Michaels.

MARCY Good, good, good. How are you today?

DR. MICHAELS And your name is?

MARCY   Marcy Smith-McMillan.

DR. MICHAELS   There are certain aspects to our arrangement that are not acceptable, Marcy. Although our net income per session from C.C. I. is slightly higher than our previous situation, it has come at the cost of extremely time-consuming redundant paperwork, telephone time on hold, telephone tag, requests for authorization, "lost in the mail" excuses, verbal authorizations that are given but not backed up in writing, along with authorizations for treatment that are rejected on the most petty grounds. So that the entire endeavour is beginning—

MARCY   I'm sorry, but could you clarify what you mean by that?

DR. MICHAELS   By what?

MARCY   "Petty".

DR. MICHAELS   Could I clarify it? The word you mean?

MARCY   I know what the word means, but I'd like you to clarify your precise use of it in regards to us.

DR. MICHAEL   I think I could do that.

MARCY   Well, I'm certain I would find that helpful, if it wouldn't be too much trouble.

DR. MICHAELS   No, no, not at all. I'd be happy to help. By "petty" I mean, in as much as—to cite one example, we have a very troubled little girl, Frannie Bascome, who we are trying to help. You're her case manager, right?

MARCY   Yes, I am.

DR. MICHAELS   So you're keenly aware of the foster mother, the pending adoption, the hard-to-imagine-stress-of-it-all, and sometimes after Frannie's had a rough session with a counselor, the foster mom needs a conference to deal with the aftermath. Which in fact just happened. She was right here, mind you, having brought the little girl to our offices. But because your guidelines won't allow two treatment sessions for this case on the same day, she has to get into her car and drive all the way home and then the next day, she has to drive all the way back—and whatever the emergency—it has to wait. Does that help you?—I hope that helps you with what I mean by "petty".

MARCY Actually it doesn't, because our guidelines have very sound reasons. They're not arbitrary, or lacking a basis in statistical fact or experience. They may be inconvenient at times, but they are solidly grounded in our long-term experience and evaluation in these matters.

Marcy wheels away with him watching, but no longer talking to her.

DR. MICHAELS What they are solidly grounded in is your goddamn indifference and your long-term experience of not having a soul. (*beat: agitated*) I want—I want Frannie and Timothy to be together. I want to see them, hear them. I want them to sing. I don't care if it's—(*addressing Frannie*) Frannie! Will you sing with Timothy?

FRANNIE Who's Timothy?

TIMOTHY Me. (*entering*) That would be me.

FRANNIE You're Timothy?

TIMOTHY Yes, I am.

FRANNIE Okay. (*moving to join Timothy*)

TIMOTHY Hello. (*almost violently looking away, and then back to her*) I want to widen my circle.

FRANNIE Okay.

Surreal lights and sound embrace Timothy, Frannie and Dr. Michaels.

DR. MICHAELS Timothy. Do you know "Row, row, row your boat, gently down the stream"?

TIMOTHY Nope.

DR. MICHAELS It's a song.

TIMOTHY   Don't know it.

DR. MICHAELS   Give it a try.

FRANNIE (*singing*)   "Row, row, row your boat, gently down the stream. Merrily, merrily, merrily, merrily, life is but a dream."

TIMOTHY   "Row, row, row your boat, gently down the stream. Merrily, merrily, merrily, merrily, life is but a dream."

FRANNIE & TIMOTHY   "Row, row, row your boat, gently down the stream. If you see a crocodile, don't forget to scream." (*They go faster, having fun*) "Row, row, row your boat, gently down the stream. If you see a crocodile, don't forget to scream."

As they yelp and laugh and flee, Barnard starts talking and coming down toward the chairs. Evangeline enters and sits in her chair, immobile.

BARNARD   So the big surprise was that I kept going. Blabbing away, Teresa driving me, even though it embarrassed her, going there. So after a while, I went on my own. Sometimes it seems okay, and then it seems maybe the most asinine thing I've ever done. This perfect stranger, you know. The first couple times I kept going back to bed when I got home, kind of stubbornly. Like "this is what I do. I go to bed. I'm Barnard and I go to bed, goddamnit. Things are grinding to a halt. I'm grinding to a halt." But then one day I lay down and I got scared I might never get up. I might just get stuck there. Because I was never going to figure out what happened with that machine and Abigail. Or why I was in bed with my guts icy cold, like I'm on a falling elevator hour after hour. I don't know. I just don't. (*Standing beside Evangeline, he studies her a second*) And she doesn't seem to know either. Sometimes I think she doesn't have a clue, the way she has this annoying habit of grabbing hold of some offhand remark. (*Moving to the opposite chair, he sits*)

EVANGELINE RYDER   How did that go exactly?

BARNARD   What?

MRS. RYDER   You were saying your mom and dad both worked in munitions plants during the war.

BARNARD That's right.

EVANGELINE RYDER And where was this?

BARNARD What does it matter? (*annoyed*) In this little town in Illinois. It was right after Pearl Harbor.

EVANGELINE RYDER That would be forty-one when the United States got into the war.

BARNARD The point is—what I meant—what I was getting at was that my dad stayed out of the army in World War Two and that's how he did it. He was a qualified welder but he had to be employed in the war effort, so working in the shipyards along with his age kept him out of the draft.

EVANGELINE RYDER And your mom?

BARNARD Mom didn't have to worry about the draft.

MRS. RYDER But she worked, too?

BARNARD (*turning to the audience*) See what I mean? We're off on some tangent. Am I supposed to just go along with it? (*back to Evangeline*) Yes. The war effort. So they both worked. Dad was in a shipyard and Mom worked nights in a munitions plant in another town maybe twenty miles away.

EVANGELINE RYDER And you were how old?

BARNARD A baby, I said. I was born in 1940, which makes me one or two when we moved down to my dad's home town.

EVANGELINE RYDER And this was nights? Your mom worked nights?

BARNARD Yes.

EVANGELINE RYDER Who took care of you?

BARNARD (*to audience*) Now I'm really getting annoyed. She's nosing around where it makes no sense. I don't see how we're going to get anywhere if she keeps this up.

EVANGELINE RYDER   I was asking if your mom worked nights.

BARNARD   And I said "yes."

EVANGELINE RYDER   And your dad?

BARNARD   Dad was gone, too, or sleeping because they had shifts around the clock. Building L.S.T.s—these landing barges for D-Day or Iwo Jima. So it was important work. Grandma would hold me and we'd look out the window, and watch Mom get into this car with all these women and they all had these scarves on their heads to tie up their hair. Sometimes—do you know what? I think I actually remember looking out that window and watching them drive off. Is that possible?

EVANGELINE RYDER   Do you think you do?

BARNARD   I don't see how I could. They tell me I carried on every time. Cried like a baby. Grandma was pretty old, in her sixties. I'm older than that now, but . . . Good Lord. Imagine that. (*gazing off*) How little we know.

EVANGELINE RYDER   What's that?

BARNARD   How little we know.

EVANGELINE RYDER   In what way? What do you mean?

BARNARD   How little we know. How little we know. (*to audience*) All of a sudden, it's obvious she's not concerned with the same things I am. This alarm goes off that, if I'm going to get to the bottom of things, I have to do it on my own. (*back to Evangeline*) So I should tell you, I've gone back to reading. But don't you worry—it's not in bed. But some of the same books, and this other one, too, that I loved without, I think, understanding it—*Zen and the Art of Motorcycle Maintenance*. That was a humdinger. But it's that *Drama of the Gifted Child* that still gets me. I saw a movie once where there was this gigantic Japanese puppet in robes and with this big loud voice, but he was empty, a bunch of big empty robes except for this little man hiding way deep inside all the robes and . . . Oh, yeah, the other day

I went out for a walk with my dog, and he ran off. There's a lot of woods where I live, and I couldn't see him. He has a collar and tags and everything but it was all just shadows and trees when out of nowhere he came running toward me. I wanted to scold him, I was so anxious, but I just hugged him and told him he was a good boy. And then when I got home, my wife and her friend Alice were in the kitchen. They were talking loud and laughing. They had four burners going with three pots and a frying pan. They were laughing and shouting Italian phrases, and the opera was playing way too loud all through the house. I didn't understand what they were doing there. The noise and their voices were overwhelming. I'm going to disappear if this doesn't stop, I thought. Why are they doing this? (*hesitating*) And I had these really murderous thoughts. I have to admit it. They were murderous. Like I could become a murderous madman. I raced up to bed and lay down and Ralphie ran with me. He's a good friend. Getting older though. You know, their lives are so short. I miss him already. Ole Ralphie. Ralpharooney.

EVANGELINE RYDER   Do you remember what you felt when you couldn't find Ralphie?

BARNARD (*to himself*)   Scared. (*and then to her*) Scared, I said. He'd been there and then he wasn't. Oh, yeah. I had the craziest dream. I bet you hear that a lot. Does anybody ever come in and say I had a really sensible dream? But this one was extra nutty. I don't know where I was or who else was there, but there was a girl dressed as a duck, a kind of Disney character duck. And she was very flirtatious and I was really happy. But then she stopped. Or maybe she didn't stop so much as I saw that she was insincere. She didn't like me and she'd been lying all along, and then I went through a door and there was Othello with a knife. And that's . . . about all I remember.

EVANGELINE RYDER   Othello? Why do you say that?

BARNARD   That it was him? Because it was.

EVANGELINE RYDER   Was he quoting Shakespeare or anything?

BARNARD   No. He was just there. I don't think he said anything.

EVANGELINE RYDER   But it was Othello?

BARNARD   It was him all right. And he had a knife. Othello with a knife.

EVANGELINE RYDER   Well . . . to be continued. (*standing, she turns and leaves*)

BARNARD (*rising and to the audience*)   That's the other annoying thing she does. I'm annoyed every darn time, because that's the way she ends a session. Doesn't she care that Othello's in the doorway in my dream, this murderous madman with a knife? She just says, "Well, to be continued." And that's it. I have to go.

He studies the audience and then the other characters who begin to exit.

Well, anyway. To be continued.

BLACKOUT

END OF ACT ONE

ACT TWO

Lights up as the characters return to their stations. Dr. Michaels sits in one chair facing Evangeline in the other. They are immobile. Slight pause before ALEX enters through the reception area door. He peeks shyly at the audience and then he addresses them.

ALEX   Hi. When I was first thinking about possibly going to the center, I thought it might be best if I wore a disguise. I was so SO nervous. I went so far as to actually create one and try it on, but in the mirror, I just looked like me with a fake mustache and *unattractive* clothes. So I thought, "I can't go like this. I can't even go out of the house looking like this." I changed back to what I like to wear, and sat in front of the television watching *Duck Dynasty* and thinking, I won't go. Or if I do go, I won't tell them anything—which made no sense—so I thought, Well, at least I won't tell them I'm gay, which made no sense. What would I tell them? And then, watching *Duck Dynasty*, I thought, "These people are crazy. They're much crazier than I am." So the next day I called to make an appointment and got one, and a couple days later, I had my first session, or initial whatever with Dr. Michaels . . . (*Having paced about he now stands between Dr. Michaels and Evangeline*) . . . and it started out okay but after a while—I don't know what it was—but he made me uncomfortable. I wasn't sure that he liked me. Not that he could or should like me—after all, I'd just walked in off the street and sat down and there I was, you know, talking about myself. He looked bored, or suspicious, or unhappy, or something, and the next thing I knew, I just stopped talking and he didn't say anything for the longest time, and I got very tired, I got very very tired and just kind of this hopeless feeling came over me, and this really painful heaviness in my chest and stomach, and before I knew I was even going to speak, I said to him, in this little voice, this very soft little voice,

"Could I maybe see a woman counsellor? Would that be possible or is it impossible?" His expression remained totally unchanged and indecipherable, but, after what in my experience anyway seemed maybe a week, or a week and a half, he said:

DR. MICHAELS "Of course, Alex. Do you think you'd like that?"

ALEX And I said, "Maybe." (*watching Dr. Michaels rise and take a step, facing out*) And he looked out the window, so I looked out the window, so we were both looking out the window when he said,

DR. MICHAELS I think you and Evangeline Ryder might work out."

Dr. Michaels exits, leaving Evangeline and Alex alone.

EVANGELINE RYDER Well, Alex, what is it that brings you to the center? If you can say. Can you say?

ALEX (*pacing anxiously behind the chair*) No. I mean, no.

EVANGELINE RYDER Have you been thinking about coming for a while or did—

ALEX I'm alone a lot. Almost all the time. My mom and dad are dead for some time now. I was in college, living at home when they died. One right after the other, and I'm an only child. So I stayed in college, and I got a room by myself and lived alone and studied the sciences—biology, which was amazing, for example with cells consuming and transforming energy, and chemistry, where I was fascinated by the interaction of substances through intermolecular forces and . . . Anyway I lived alone and I'm still alone. Sometimes I get so mad at everything and everybody—not you—but I envy everybody who has someone in their lives—I see people on the street walking together and I hate them. Is that weird? Do you feel that way ever?

EVANGELINE RYDER It doesn't matter how I feel, but how you feel, Alex.

ALEX Well, that's how I feel. Not all the time—I was watching *Duck Dynasty*, those crazy men—you know, those men, those rough, bearded men—they're men, you know, they hunt and kill things and I'm gay. (*he gasps, freezes, startled*) Okay, okay. I said it. Oh, my god. I said it.

EVANGELINE RYDER   Yes, you did.

ALEX   I didn't mean to say it. It just came out. I was talking and all of a sudden I felt—she knows. Tell her. Had you guessed? I bet you had.

EVANGELINE RYDER   I hadn't really thought about it.

ALEX   Is it okay?

EVANGELINE RYDER   What?

ALEX   That I'm gay and you know it. Will you still see me?

EVANGELINE RYDER   Of course.

ALEX   Oh, that's wonderful.

EVANGELINE RYDER   Did you worry I wouldn't?

ALEX   Everybody says it's okay—come out—it's okay, but then there's all those others who hate—(*moving to sit*)—you can feel it, they just hate, like those *Duck Dynasty* men—can I ask you something?

EVANGELINE RYDER   If you want.

ALEX   Are you gay? Are you?

EVANGELINE RYDER   We don't talk about ourselves, Alex.

ALEX   But are you?

EVANGELINE RYDER   I'm sorry. I can't say.

ALEX   Oh. Okay. I'm sorry. Maybe I shouldn't have asked. Is it wrong that I asked?

EVANGELINE RYDER   It would only be wrong if I answered. How long have you felt this way?

ALEX   Oh, forever. But do you know what? I have no experience. None. Although I'm working on it—going to gay bars and—Is that all right, do you think?

EVANGELINE RYDER   Of course. But you've had no experience?

ALEX   No. Honest. I'm being one hundred percent honest. Because I don't think that violin teacher in grade school, Mr. Schultz, counts. Because that was pretty much his experience. Except for Tommy Augustine in his tree house but he wouldn't speak to me after, and crossed the street to avoid me from that day on. He liked to play baseball. He was good, too. I saw him hit it far sometimes.

EVANGELINE RYDER   And the violin teacher—? Do you still play the violin?

ALEX   Oh, no.

EVANGELINE RYDER   Did you stop because of what happened?

ALEX   Oh, no. My mom and dad wanted me to play. But I had enough trouble without getting known as the sissy who liked long-hair music. Sissy was bad enough.

EVANGELINE RYDER   Do you think the fact that Mr. Shultz—

ALEX   No. Absolutely not. He was just sad. He was just silly. Everybody made fun of him. I never think of him. Tommy wanted to grow up and be straight, and I think he did. He got married, I know. I never blamed him. I would have done the same thing, if I could have.

EVANGELINE RYDER   Done what?

ALEX   Stopped.

EVANGELINE RYDER   Stopped?

ALEX   Yes. You know. Stopped being gay. Stopped being Alex. Wouldn't anybody?

Alex spins his chair away.

EVANGELINE RYDER (*spinning, facing out*)   What a first session! Wow!

They propel their chairs in opposite directions, Alex and Evangeline ending in reverse places in changing light, as they start a new session.

ALEX (*almost luxuriating*)   I think you're the most wonderful, marvelous therapist in the whole United States of America. Or maybe on planet earth. Or the whole crazy universe. I love seeing you. I want to tell you everything. I'm in love. I didn't mention it before because I wanted to be sure. But I've had this wonderful man in my life almost a month.

EVANGELINE RYDER   Really?

ALEX   Yes. This sweet darling man—he's a little paunchy, but in a cute way, and my guess is he's a weekender—a kind of distinguished, executive type, but it's been uncanny—the wavelength we share— from the first instant. He touched his glass—he was drinking a gin and tonic and he slid the glass along the bar—not able to look at me—and when the glass had moved about a foot, he brought it back and cradled it in both palms, raising it ever so slowly to his mouth to drink. And since then, since that first moment, everything has only gotten deeper. Even though on the second weekend he was a little shy, but then on the third, when I would stare at him—not rudely, but discretely, covertly, he started to loosen his tie and tighten his tie, and loosen it, and I thought, "Oh, heavens, the poor thing, he's so nervous—" and then he turned, his fingers still toying with the knot—and I swear it was like he was touching me—and he looked at me. And I thought, "Oh, god, so this is it, so this is what love is like, this is what it feels like not to be alone." His eyes were beyond description.

EVANGELINE RYDER   He's a weekender, you say?

ALEX   That's my guess.

EVANGELINE RYDER   But you don't know? Has he refused to tell you?

ALEX   I haven't asked. We don't talk.

EVANGELINE RYDER   Not about anything? His work, or—

ALEX   We have no need to talk. (*eyeing her*) I know it's strange, or seems strange, but its wonderful. That's the wonder of it. When he looked at me, I don't have the words and I never will, I couldn't stand it. I got up and walked away—out the door, out to my car. And I drove away with the radio playing Drake's "Hold On, We're Going Home," as loud as I could—louder than I'd ever played anything before in my life. I don't think I can survive until next Saturday—until I see him again, because I will—I know it, and something will happen—I don't know what, but—more will happen. Something wonderful.

Alex goes and Evangeline spins toward the desk to find Dr. Michaels entering with two drinks.

EVANGELINE RYDER   Bob. Thanks be to you. (*taking one of the drinks, as he settles on the piano bench*) Cheers and blessings. That young man you sent me, Alex—he's gay—and I have to say parenthetically—his sweetness is like that of a newborn. (*sitting on the bench beside him*) I had to fight not to burst into tears when he left our first session. But we're at it a while now, and today he was telling me about a love interest. Which seemed off somehow and made me nervous and then worried because the more he spoke the clearer it became that this lover must be imaginary. I mean, the man is probably real and really in the bar where Alex sees him, but I think Alex's relationship is a complete fantasy.

DR. MICHAELS   Are you certain? I mean, if this is the first time he spoke of the relationship?

EVANGELINE RYDER   He's been leading me to it. Even as he celebrated the fantasy, he offered clues aplenty to the fact that it isn't real.

DR. MICHAELS   Is it possible he's on the verge of psychosis, do you think?

EVANGELINE RYDER   I need to stay alert, but I suspect this is more an attempt to prop up very fragile, almost infantile self-esteem.

DR. MICHAELS If he's sharing all this—letting you participate—these are reparative fantasies—then he's counting on you in ways he may not even know.

EVANGELINE RYDER But I do. So just be there and be patient, Evangeline.

DR. MICHAELS Let his trust guide yours.

EVANGELINE RYDER Just be and not be. Be what he needs, but not too much. Piece of cake.

As they sip their drinks.

DR. MICHAELS I'm trying to white knuckle it myself with this Frannie Bascome situation. But sometimes I'd like to bring her home. Before the system—me included—grinds her into dust. Just take care of her. You know, like I'm the three bears.

EVANGELINE RYDER You're not a bear, Bob.

DR. MICHAELS Or maybe the seven dwarfs.

EVANGELINE RYDER I was at a dinner party last week. You know, convivial. Lots of chatter. Everybody upright. Sane. All that. And then the host got it into his head that I should see something. He took me up this narrow stairway to the attic in his two hundred year old home. "I thought this might interest you," he said. "Given your line of work." The dining room, where the guests we'd left were laughing over desert under us, had a fireplace with a chimney that came up though the attic floor and went out the roof. What he wanted to show me was a path worn into the floorboards. It circled the chimney, an actual dent rubbed into the wood by the feet of someone walking in a circle, someone who years ago had been confined in that attic, someone with a mental illness, kept out of sight for days, months, years. The country gentleman smiled and said, "Interesting, no?" I said, "Yes," and we went down for some apple pie. But I carried that lost figure with me—man or woman—I don't know which—but a banished soul. Imagine such a fate. Alone up there hearing the dinner parties, all the life below. Fleeing demons, pursuing hope, getting nowhere. Disappearing, finally. Nothing left but a scar in those two hundred-year-old planks. (*beat*) You know— that phantom, I felt compelled to bring down from that attic—that's what you're feeling—you want to take Frannie out of the hellhole she's in. But you can't get involved. I don't know what you're thinking, but whatever it is, it's really not an option. You know what I'm saying.

DR. MICHAELS (*nodding, then looking up at Mom.*)   It's my Mom I see sometimes like that. Pacing around our apartment while I'm out. Playing. Or at school.

The reception room door swings open and Alex rushes in to stand at his therapy chair, as Evangeline moves back to her chair.

ALEX   He didn't show up. I was in the right place. I waited, and I drank, and I drank too much, and then I remembered how the last time I saw him, he'd turned away to light his cigarette in this way that I hadn't understood then, but now saw was a sign of his sudden dislike of me. And then he'd raised his drink ever so slowly to a height that declared his absolute and final rejection of me. I don't know what I did. I really don't. I was so careful, so thoughtful with him. I'm being honest, Evangeline.

EVANGELINE RYDER   I know you are.

ALEX   It's unbearable, really. I'm feeling just awful, you know.

EVANGELINE RYDER   I can see that, Alex. How do you think he's dealing with it all?

ALEX   Who?

EVANGELINE RYDER   The weekender? Is he missing you? What's his name, anyway?

ALEX   Oh, he doesn't care. He doesn't even know I exist.

EVANGELINE RYDER   What do you mean?

ALEX   Ohhh . . . (*in small but angry voice, he tells her*) Shut up.

EVANGELINE RYDER   It's literally true isn't it.

ALEX   What? (*again that voice*) Shut up, shut up.

EVANGELINE RYDER   That he doesn't know you exist.

ALEX   It's just so impossible. Reality. Reality. This big, noisy, crazy onrush of everything. Stuff, of things. People. I don't know what to do.

EVANGELINE RYDER   It's all right.

ALEX   No. (*beat*) Is it? It's so scary to do things, you know.

EVANGELINE RYDER   It's good that you told me. I'm grateful you were honest. I'm wondering if we might consider prescribing some kind of medication.

ALEX   Like what?

EVANGELINE RYDER   I was thinking along the lines of Prozac.

ALEX   Prozac? For me? Why? Can I think about it?

EVANGELINE RYDER   Of course. But I believe it would help you level out and make this easier to get through.

ALEX   You've been thinking about this haven't you. You've been thinking about me and Prozac for a while. You've been onto me. Way ahead of me. Oh, that's so wonderful. You know me. Thank you, thank you. Okay, okay, okay. Prozac schmozac, Evangeline. If you say so, yes. Yes, I'll do it, yes. Gimme me the whole cornucopia.

Alex turns and goes, as Evangeline exits, and the space turns surreal with lights and sound. Frannie enters, looking around and then she addresses the audience, carefully, warily, looking for help.

FRANNIE   Even though they say my name over and over, I don't know who they're talking about, or if it's maybe me they're talking about. Because do you know what happened? It's a secret kind of mystery, as far as I can tell, but long ago, way before everything, I was taken out of my mom and dad's house—I don't know why or even how—and they put me in a different house and then I got taken out of that house with those people and carried back to where Dad

166

was gone, and then I got grabbed and put in a different house and brought back when Mom was with Steve, and . . . they took me and she was with Zach, and they took me, took me, took me, and she was with Gregory and that's now. And this is not some cardboard cut-out story I'm telling about with gingerbread woods and bread crumbs, or trolls with spooky names but my very very very real life. Not that I remember it, because I don't; but there's all these bouncy sort of pictures and big noises and spooky colors and the sky getting dark and darker and black.

Mom enters behind Frannie who does not see her at this instant.

Which I don't think anybody could say is a memory I'm remembering, least of all me. (*turning, seeing Mom*) But the storm does. The storm remembers every little tiny second.

MOM   Who are you talking to?

FRANNIE   I'm just talking. It was to nobody. I was talking to nobody.

MOM   Do you talk to nobody often?

FRANNIE   All the time. That's who I'm always talking to.

MOM   I am nobody.

FRANNIE   That's funny.

MOM   No, I am. I'm nobody and I'm nothing.

FRANNIE   That's funny.

MOM   Shall we go for a walk? (*offering her hand*)

FRANNIE   Okay. (*approaching carefully*) Do you know any pretty songs?

MOM (*offering her hand*)   Of course.

As Frannie takes her hand, they go off holding hands, as a phone starts ringing.

NORA (*standing and frantic*)   I can't find her. Damnit, I can't find her.

DR. MICHAELS What do you mean?

NORA I don't know where the hell she is. I can't handle this any more. I really—

DR. MICHAELS Wait, Nora! What happened? Where is she?

NORA I don't know. I fell asleep. God forgive me but shouldn't I be able to get a little sleep? We don't sleep here anymore. You have no idea what's been going on.

DR. MICHAELS Have you called the police?

NORA I called you.

DR. MICHAELS We have to call the police. Is she really missing?

NORA I called you.

DR. MICHAELS Have you looked everywhere?

NORA It's a tiny apartment, Dr. Michaels. I woke up like somebody shrieked in my ear, and my purse was dumped and money gone. Not my credit cards or keys or— I staggered out and it was all over the kitchen floor—

As Dr. Michaels has turned away to root in documents on the desk, Denise enters through the reception door behind him and she has Frannie with her.

DENISE Bob, Bob—

DR. MICHAELS No, no, Denise, not—(*and turning he sees Frannie*) She's here. Nora.

NORA What? Who? Are you talking to me?

DENISE I just happened to look out and she was climbing out of the back of a pickup truck.

DR. MICHAELS Frannie's here, Nora.

NORA She's where? There? She's with you?

DR. MICHAELS She hitchhiked. Get over here as fast as you can.

NORA Jesus god almighty.

DR. MICHAELS Hey. Frannie. Hi. What's up?

FRANNIE I wanted to look at that book some more. (*approaching*)

DR. MICHAELS What book?

FRANNIE The one I was reading. It was about trolls.

Barnard starts talking as the others all go and he comes down to the main playing area.

BARNARD Anyway, I should have brought this up sooner today, but everything else got in the way, though I don't understand how. Because driving over I was just about bursting with what happened and sure it would be the first words out of my mouth. But then I rambled on about—Damnit, I'm doing it again. I go grocery shopping when I leave here. Cerutti's Market. It's on the way home, and so I went last Wednesday. I go about it in a certain way. I come in the door into the vegetables and fruit. I have a list. So I put apples and oranges in my cart. Bananas. I took some cabbage and salad stuff, and as I came around a corner, there was this girl and it was clear she worked there; she was restocking the shelves, and I thought how she was attractive. I'd never seen her before, so I figured she was new. I had more shopping, bread, cereal, and then I came to where I needed this special toothpaste that the website said this store carried. But I couldn't find it. So I glanced over to the little cubbyhole where the person in charge of this section sometimes is and it was the girl who had crossed my path. She was at this little table. So I asked her about the toothpaste and she said they did carry it and went over to show me. We were looking at the shelves and we were talking and she was right next to me, and her face was so close that when I looked at her she was blurry. But the toothpaste wasn't there and she recommended this other brand. But it was funny. There was something funny about it. I continued shopping and whenever I caught sight of her, she seemed more attractive than ever in this special way, and I just gazed at her almost like she was a natural wonder. The checkout line there is usually fast, but the woman ahead of me was talking about a bake sale and about having Lyme disease and the antibiotic she was taking. I just wanted to get going. But then I noticed that that girl was crouched down to refill those shelves that they have up by the checkout lanes. I was unloading my cart, but watching her. I'd been very careful up till then not to look for too long. Her back was toward me as she stood and started away. I was watching her very closely when she turned her head sharply around to look over her shoulder right at me. And it was this deep knowing look right into my eyes. She knew I'd been watching her all along, and then she turned and walked on, and her body language had this quality of—it reminded me of these elk I'd seen on TV and the males, the rams head-butted each other in mating season, and then the ram who won followed the female elk into the mountains, and she would look over her shoulder at him every now and then, and then keep going. And it felt like that sort of, the body language, her looking over her shoulder, and walking on seemed to say, "Here I am, and I'm going this way. I'll be over here."

beat

Well, I had no intention of doing anything, so I was laughing to myself. But as I drove home, I couldn't stop thinking about her. I felt like I had to go back. I felt I was hurting her, I was disappointing her if I didn't go back. I didn't even know her, but I felt like I was losing her. Driving my car, or shaving, it was all for her. That's why I was doing these things. And I would tell myself that it was ridiculous. But the feeling didn't care. I couldn't rest.

EVANGELINE RYDER   And this is someone you never saw before?

BARNARD   Never. I think she must have been hired recently. At home, I started feeling really tired and irritable. I went to bed in the middle of the afternoon. Fortunately, my wife was out, or she'd have started in on me, for sure. I managed to get up for dinner. But I felt awful.

EVANGELINE RYDER   You said earlier there was one moment where you felt something funny?

BARNARD When we were looking for the toothpaste. That's when—(*suddenly frightened*) I mean, what if it doesn't stop? What if I lay down and I don't get up until I'm dead. I mean, I won't get up then. But what if that's the next thing that happens—I'm dead, and that's the thing that has to happen to make the icy feeling stop.

EVANGELINE RYDER Let's not let that happen, you and I. How is it now? On a scale of one to ten.

BARNARD That feeling? It's okay. Six? Maybe five even?

EVANGELINE RYDER Okay. I'm wondering about that moment—is there anything more you can say? Could you be more specific?

BARNARD What moment? The funny one?

EVANGELINE RYDER Yes.

BARNARD I don't see how. Funny. Peculiar. And so what I did the next day is I made up some excuse and drove back to the store. I didn't buy much because I'd just shopped, but I picked up some carrots and blueberries and made my way toward her area, like there was something dangerous hiding there. And when I got close and saw her, it was the damndest thing. Because I wasn't sure it was the same girl. I couldn't really tell if it was or it wasn't.

EVANGELINE RYDER Really.

BARNARD No. I couldn't. She was at her little desk doing paperwork—but I was dumbfounded. Honest to god, I couldn't tell. She had the same black hair, though in a different style, and her clothes were different, but it was a day later, so of course she changed her clothes. So I went off but came right back worried that if she saw me, she might think I was stalking her. I was stalking her, I guess. I have all this white hair sticking up over the shelves that she might recognize. Then this other man came along and he said to her, "That was a really delicious meal the other night." And she said, "Thanks. I'd really like to do a lot more catering." And just hearing them was a kind of relief. I don't know why.

EVANGELINE RYDER   I think it was grounding. It put her into an ordinary context.

BARNARD   I guess. Maybe. But something else happened. I decided to get the heck out of there, and I grabbed some bars of soap, but when I pushed my cart clear of the aisles, she was right in front of me. And she saw me and looked at me and said "Hi," and I said "Hi" and I couldn't see her.

EVANGELINE RYDER   What do you mean?

BARNARD   I *could* . . . *not* . . . see her. It was just this blur. Or more like light, really, but there we were, and she was stocking shelves, and I was looking at her out of this—out of this—vortex—this whirlwind out of which I couldn't see. It was like she was in the middle of a lightning bolt. Or she was a lightning bolt. I just went on and checked out and drove home.

EVANGELINE RYDER   And you really never recognized her for sure, as the same girl?

BARNARD   No.

EVANGELINE RYDER   But it was the same girl?

BARNARD   I don't know if it was or it wasn't. I think it was.

EVANGELINE RYDER   I'm wondering something. We're almost out of time, but . . .

BARNARD   What?

EVANGELINE RYDER   We may not have enough time to get into this.

BARNARD   No, no. What?

EVANGELINE RYDER   Do you remember a while ago—we started talking about when you lived with your grandparents in that little Illinois town?

BARNARD   (*deeply puzzled*)   What? (*turning out*) Oh, no. Here we go again.

172

EVANGELINE RYDER   Your mom went away to work every night.

BARNARD   Dad, too.

EVANGELINE RYDER   Your grandmother held you and you cried watching your mom go. You watched her get into a car with all these women with scarves on their heads.

BARNARD   Mom and those women wore scarves—babushkas— because they had to keep their hair back. They worked with explosives.

As Mom, wearing 1940s clothing and a scarf on her head approaches Barnard.

EVANGELINE RYDER   That girl looked at you, and then she walked away.

BARNARD   I said that.

EVANGELINE RYDER   Your mother would go and return, and it's transforming every time. And in both directions. To the infant, his mother is everything. The world.

BARNARD   What do you mean?

EVANGELINE RYDER   It's transforming.

BARNARD   What is?

As Mom stands before him, between him and Evangeline.

EVANGELINE RYDER   Her presence, her eyes, her warmth. You transformed when she arrived in one way—that way—and then you transformed in another way when she left.

BARNARD   Transform in what way? You said transform and I'm thinking "in what way?" I'm really nervous. Transform in what way?

EVANGELINE RYDER   There's a book—you like books—the ostensible subject is photography. The writer wants to identify exactly how a photograph sits in time as a single instant that affects us. How certain photographs pierce us. But along the way he starts writing about his mother who has just died and who he lived with for the last twenty-six years. He's been going through all the photographs he has of her, looking for one that will pierce him. He knows he is supposed to grieve for her death, and then move on, but he writes he's not going to do that. Because she is irreplaceable. Not indispensable, but irreplaceable. And so to accept the loss is not possible. It makes no sense. He keeps looking through the pictures and the one he finally settles on—the one that pierces him, and which he does not include in the book because he believes his readers would not see it as he does—that photo is of his mother when she was five years old. (*rising*) I'm sorry, but . . . Well, to be continued.

BARNARD   I don't think I should go shopping today.

EVANGELINE RYDER   Why?

BARNARD   What? (*jumping up*) How can you ask? She works there. What if I see her? She knows I was looking at her.

Dr. Michaels enters watching Barnard, as Evangeline leaves.

I know. I know. To be continued. But that's what I'm afraid of. That it'll just go on and on.

DR. MICHAELS   Barnard. (*as Barnard looks, Dr. Michaels turns to Jane at her station*) Jane. I think Barnard really needs a song.

JANE   Hey. Barnard.

BARNARD   What?

JANE   Want to sing with us?

JEROME   I do, Jane. (*heading to the piano*)

BARNARD (*crankily*)   I don't know who you are. Any of you.

ALEX (*arriving*)   I'd like to.

As others arrive, Mrs. Garland and Jimmy who carries the shotgun.

JANE   It's Dr. Michaels idea, Barnard. You know you want to.

BARNARD   No, I don't. I don't know that. You and who? Oh, it doesn't matter. I don't want to do it. I don't feel like it. I feel like going to bed.

JIMMY   Barnard, I promise you—you'll be sorry if you don't.

MRS. GARLAND   He's gonna miss out.

DR. MICHAELS   Give a try, Barnard. Jimmy's doing it—he's singing, and he's dead.

BARNARD   No. No, darn you all. Lemme alone.

JEROME   Here we go.

Jerome starts playing and they sing and maybe dance.

JANE, JIMMY, MRS. GARLAND, JEROME, ALEX, DR. MICHAELS
Nothing could be finer than to be in Carolina in the mor-or-or-ning. No one could be sweeter than my sweetie when I meet her in the mor-or-or-ning. If I had Aladdin's lamp for only a day, I'd make a wish and here's what I'd say: Nothing could be finer than to be in Carolina in the mor-or-or-ning.

Lights abruptly change as Frannie and Nora, speaking immediately, make they way to the main area.

NORA   It's out of control. It's broken. Sometimes you just break. I'm broken. We haven't slept in three days—no, four days—who knows—five, six—seven? She started urinating in her room. In the corner and, she defecated, too. At least it's the corner. I should be grateful. Even though the bathroom is right outside the door. The first time I thought it was an accident, or just something that wouldn't happen again. But it's almost constant now.

They are with Dr. Michaels. Frannie sits bowed over, collapsed in her chair.

DR. MICHAELS   What about the change in medication? Would you say it's helped?

NORA   This is the worst it's ever been. Whatever that proves.

DR. MICHAELS We've got to remember it's only two weeks until the final hearing on terminating the birth mother's rights, and once that happens—

NORA You say that like two weeks is nothing. She hitchhiked over here to see you, didn't she. In a pickup truck.

DR. MICHAELS Yes she did.

NORA Why? She ran away from me.

FRANNIE To read my book.

NORA What if she died or got killed doing that, whose fault would that be? She walked out of my apartment and stood on the side of the road with her thumb out and got into the back of a pickup truck while I was home sleeping. I don't think I can do this any more.

DR. MICHAELS Of course you can.

NORA What do you mean—of course I can. Maybe I can't.

DR. MICHAELS There's something we can do. There's a way to get help until the hearing, and once they terminate the birth mother's rights, I promise you—

NORA You mean *if* they terminates her rights.

DR. MICHAELS They will. They have to.

NORA No they don't have to and we both know that. I don't think I can stand what's going on for another day let alone two weeks.

DR. MICHAELS You're just feeling exhausted and not thinking straight and it's no wonder—

NORA Don't tell me what I'm thinking. Please.

DR. MICHAELS Nora. There's a solution. I've spoken to Protective Services now, and they feel and I feel that a period of psychiatric hospitalization for Frannie is appropriate. Would you agree to that?

FRANNIE (*peeking up*) Do they know about storms there?

DR. MICHAELS What Frannie?

FRANNIE In this hospital is it a storm hospital? Do they know about storms, because the storms will come with me.

NORA Have you spoken to Colossal Care? Will they approve hospitalization?

DR. MICHAELS They have to. It's their responsibility.

NORA But have you spoken to them?

DR. MICHAELS I have a call in to her case manager. I've faxed my updated report and recommendation and Protective Services has done the same, backing me one hundred percent.

FRANNIE Tell them I'm bringing lots and lots of storms.

DR. MICHAELS All right, Frannie. I will.

FRANNIE They better be ready. Because sometimes when the storm is scarier than a big mean bear got me in his mouth, or a crocodile, or a lion or tiger, or snake eating me up—

NORA I can't do this anymore. (*sinking to the floor, taking up the downward-facing dog yoga pose*)

DR. MICHAELS You have to.

NORA Okay. Is there any coffee? (*moving into the "down dog" pose*)

FRANNIE They better have toothpicks, or a paper clips, because the blood coming out of me makes the storms go away. So they better be ready. Do they have nails or paper clips or knives?

DR. MICHAELS You won't need those things there, Frannie. I promise. We're all she has, Nora. You and me.

NORA Okay.

As Denise pops in the reception area door.

DENISE C.C.I., Bob. Line six.

Marcy appears. Frannie sits bowed over, Nora is in her yoga pose near Frannie.

MARCY Hello, hello.

DR. MICHAELS Hello.

MARCY (*cheery and helpful*) Dr. Michaels. How are you today? Good, I hope.

DR. MICHAELS Sorry to have kept you waiting, Marcy.

MARCY No problem. But in the name of not getting too far down the wrong road I want to make it clear that our very best people have given a thorough reassessment of all the reports on this Frannie Bascome and Colossal Care cannot do what your asking. It's our determination that psychiatric hospitalization is not medically necessary at this point.

DR. MICHAELS You read my most recent report.

MARCY Of course. We've read all the reports. I said that.

As Marcy and Dr. Michaels begin to prowl and talk.

DR. MICHAELS And that's your determination?

MARCY That's our firm determination.

DR. MICHAELS Because I disagree totally. I disagree as forcefully as—

MARCY I think I said, it's our "firm" determination.

DR. MICHAELS I understand that but this child is suicidal. And a hospital stay—

MARCY I told you, Dr. Michaels, I read the report.

DR. MICHAELS But with a hospital stay she could learn that when she can't control herself, there are safe places for her to go. The foster mother would be able to see that there's help when things go out of control. And they could rest. They both need some rest.

MARCY Here's what we're recommending. We're recommending that you table the hospital idea and substitute an increase in the frequency of sessions.

DR. MICHAELS But this child is in a state of—

MARCY Needing rest simply does not meet the criteria of Medical Necessity required for hospitalization.

DR. MICHAELS To how many? Increase the frequency of sessions to how many?

MARCY As many as you see fit.

DR. MICHAELS It would be at my discretion.

MARCY Well, you're the on-site caregiver.

DR. MICHAELS Will you put that in writing?

MARCY What?

DR. MICHAELS What you just said. What you just told me.

MARCY And what was that?

DR. MICHAELS What was what?

MARCY What did I say?

DR. MICHAELS You're asking me to tell you what you said?

MARCY I'm asking, "What do you think I said? What do you think I said?"

DR. MICHAELS What you said, and what I think you said, and what I want you to put into writing is that you are authorizing me to determine the frequency of sessions necessary in this case.

MARCY I don't understand.

DR. MICHAELS What? What don't you understand?

MARCY I can't possibly do what you're asking—give you carte blanche on the frequency of sessions.

DR. MICHAELS   So you're saying that's not what you said.

MARCY   I would have to. Because there would have to be a complete reevaluation of the case before such a radical authorization could even be considered.

DR. MICHAELS   I can all but guarantee you—I'm absolutely certain those were not the words you used a few minutes ago.

MARCY   Probably not, because in those circumstances, as I understood them, what I was doing—or trying to do, is not what I'm doing now.

DR. MICHAELS   What are you doing now?

MARCY   What am I doing? (*as if she doesn't quite know*) Well, I'm—I mean, what I'm doing doesn't matter, because the guidelines on this question are detailed and unequivocal and as firm as possible.

DR. MICHAELS   So you're not authorizing what I thought.

MARCY   Not if you thought that.

DR. MICHAELS   Then what are you authorizing?

MARCY   Well, that you see the patient as often as you deem necessary, using your best judgement, and being as scrupulous as possible and responsible to all our interests, taking everything into consideration, and then just submit requests to us for reimbursement.

DR. MICHAELS   Which you may or may not accept.

MARCY   Right. It will depend on whether or not they qualify according to the guidelines.

DR. MICHAELS   I see. Well, there's no need to put that in writing.

MARCY   No. That's already in writing. Which is why we have the guidelines. To eliminate this kind of confusion.

DR. MICHAELS   So you're turning us down.

MARCY   Not really. No, no. We offered what we offered. Now feel free to call us if you have further questions. (*starting to depart*)

DR. MICHAELS Wait a minute. Do you have another minute? I want to tell you something. I want you to understand something.

MARCY All right. But time is limited. I don't have forever.

DR. MICHAELS None of us do. But this is the larger view. Do you have a minute for the larger view?

MARCY Of course.

DR. MICHAELS Nobody walks in our door to pass the time of day. People come here so stressed they fear they're losing their mind. So we need to be here and ready. But short term. Always short term. Eight sessions if they're lucky. Our "Adult Outpatient" service is available regardless of income, or insurance, or severity of problem. But the state restricts mental health funding for adults—meaning our payment—to people with chronic mental illness. Which forces us to rely on companies like yours, or at times to triage those who most need our help. And so—now this is the part I want you to hear—are you listening?

MARCY Indeed I am. And waiting, too, because you have yet to tell me anything I'm not keenly aware of.

Facing each other at some distance.

DR. MICHAELS I'm building to it, Marcy—that's what's coming now—something I doubt you have ever thought of. So you just keep it in mind, Marcy—because should you get fired from your nice job at C.C.I., and end up depressed because you can't cope, and slash your wrists and get taken to the hospital, the hospital will get paid for stitching you up; but if you decide as a result of nearly dying by your own hand that you'd better get some outpatient care before you try it again, you're going to have to pay for that the best way you can, or the best way the "guidelines" of whatever insurance company you have permits. Or be at our mercy. You got all that?

MARCY I think I do.

DR. MICHAELS Now I know you're desperate to get away from me, but I just have to ask—are you aware that the stockholders at C.C.I.

were so happy with the company's performance last year that they rewarded the C.E.O. with a fifty million dollar–one-time bonus?

MARCY I did know that. Isn't it wonderful. (*heading off*) But I better get back to work before I get fired. (*stopping, looking back*) And Dr. Michaels—about you and your sense of the larger view? I think you lost track of it.

DR. MICHAELS Well, thank you for noticing, Marcy.

MARCY No problem. Anytime.

She exits, and Dr. Michaels turns to go as Timothy and Evangeline enter, talking. Evangeline sits while Timothy, who is agitated, paces.

TIMOTHY Turn the other cheek. That's what I do. Bury the hatchet. That's what I do. WHY ARE YOU TAKING THEIR SIDE WHEN YOU SHOULD BE ON MY SIDE?

EVANGELINE RYDER I'm not on anybody's side, Timothy, but you were rude with what you did, the way you interrupted their checkers.

TIMOTHY I DIDN'T. They were mean to me first. I WANTED TO TELL THEM SOMETHING AND THEY WOULDN'T LET ME.

EVANGELINE RYDER Your father says they told him you kicked the table, spilling the checkers and everything.

TIMOTHY I said I was sorry. Live and let live. Let bygones be bygones. THEY SHOULD TRY A LITTLE KINDNESS.

EVANGELINE RYDER But you can't be mean to them that way.

TIMOTHY You stop it. You're not so perfect and everybody can find out. I'll go door to door and tell everybody. I'll put it in the newspaper. I'll go and become a homeless person without a home living out in the—IN THE AIR. THEY'RE ALL MEAN TO ME, AND IT'S MY MOM AND DAD'S HOUSE, AND BOB IS

DAD'S FRIEND, AND TOM IS BOB'S FRIEND. BECAUSE
THEY'RE ALL MEAN.

EVANGELINE RYDER (*suddenly pretending anger*)   You know what
Timothy? You're one hundred percent right. They're a bunch of
jerks. THAT'S WHAT THEY ARE. JERKS. AND DOPES, AND
THE NEXT TIME YOU SEE THOSE GUYS, YOU TELL THEM
TO GO SUCK EGGS!

TIMOTHY   Whoa now. Take it easy.

EVANGELINE RYDER   No, no. Why should I? They deserve it, and
they should know it. Let's go together right now and tell them they
are all stupid jerks.

TIMOTHY   Take it easy. Take it easy.

EVANGELINE RYDER   No. I'm mad. I'm really, really mad. I want to
do something about this right now. Every one of them is a jerk and
they should straighten up and fly right. They should take a long walk
on a short pier.

TIMOTHY   GET A HOLD OF YOURSELF, EVANGELINE.

EVANGELINE RYDER   No, I can't. You're so upset. They hurt your
feelings.

TIMOTHY   I just wanted to talk to them. But you gotta calm down.
I want to advise you to calm down. You're out of control. It does
nobody any good.

EVANGELINE RYDER   If you say so. All right. You're probably right.

TIMOTHY   I'm extra upset because of Otto, you know. And I
wanted to tell them. But if you're so crazy it won't help anyone.

EVANGELINE RYDER   Timothy, why are you upset about Otto?

TIMOTHY   I told you. He has to have surgery.

EVANGELINE RYDER   You didn't tell me, Timothy.

TIMOTHY   I DID TOO.

EVANGELINE RYDER   Well, maybe I forgot.

TIMOTHY   I THINK YOU DID.

EVANGELINE RYDER   He has to have surgery?

TIMOTHY   Yes. In his intestines, they call them. You've heard of them.

EVANGELINE RYDER   Yes, I have.

TIMOTHY   And they use a knife, you know. And they cut him open and everything. It's terrifying to use the right word, I think. They have to do it, or he'll—you know. And I wanted to tell Bob and Bob's friend, Tom, but they kept playing checkers. Because he's a hamster and that's nothing, but they're jerks.

EVANGELINE RYDER   Yes, they are.

TIMOTHY   They don't care. Nobody cares.

EVANGELINE RYDER   I'm really glad you told me. Because I care.

TIMOTHY   But you forgot. Do you think Otto knows?

EVANGELINE RYDER   Knows what? That it's coming? The surgery? No, no. He doesn't.

TIMOTHY   Yesterday my brother dropped me off at my parents' and my mother's friend was visiting, and we were all in the kitchen, and when we all went to look out the window at Virginia's new car, my mother's friend's dog, whose name is Arnold, ate my sandwich. I got very mad, because I was hungry but I didn't know who to be mad at, because I didn't know whose fault it was. And Virginia said it was her fault because it was her dog. I said maybe it was my fault because I didn't take my sandwich with me. Then Virginia said it was the dog's fault. And I thought I'd ask you. Whose fault was it?

EVANGELINE RYDER   You've thought a lot about this.

TIMOTHY   Yes. Can it be the dog's fault?

EVANGELINE RYDER   In a way. I think the dog knew he should not eat that sandwich.

TIMOTHY   He did? Can dogs know that? Can dogs know the difference?

EVANGELINE RYDER   That he should not eat that sandwich that was not in his bowl. Yes.

TIMOTHY   Oh, my goodness. Oh, my goodness.

EVANGELINE RYDER   What? Oh, my goodness what? Timothy.

Timothy rushes away.

Timothy. Oh, my goodness what? Timothy wait.

As she gathers herself to pursue Timothy, Dr. Michaels comes in.

DR. MICHAELS   Timothy just ran down the hall, yelling.

EVANGELINE RYDER (*starting to go*)   Sorry. He got very upset—he has a pet Hamster, Otto—and the hamster has to go into surgery, and—

DR. MICHAELS   His what? His hamster?

EVANGELINE RYDER   His pet hamster, Otto. For good or ill Otto is Timothy's strongest, most sustaining relationship, and now, well—to use his word—he's "terrified."

DR. MICHAELS   What's wrong with him?

EVANGELINE RYDER   He's anxious and having nightmares, and —

DR. MICHAELS   I mean, the hamster.

EVANGELINE RYDER   It's a blockage in his stomach, and I'm afraid something could go wrong. It would shatter Timothy, and now I think Timothy is worried that Otto knows the surgery is coming.

DR. MICHAELS   How would he know? He's a hamster.

EVANGELINE RYDER   I'll tell you later. I better see where Timothy is. The van from the home isn't due to pick him up for another ten minutes.

185

She goes. Dr. Michaels, alone, eyes the audience

DR. MICHAELS   Ahh, yes. Oh my goodness the hamster is having surgery. And does he know? Who the hell cares?

As he crosses to the piano for a drink, lights take him to home. Mom looks down from her station high and behind him.

MOM   Well, that was appalling, Robert. Really. What is wrong with you?

DR. MICHAELS   I hope you're not going to pretend you care about Timothy Archer's hamster. (*pouring a drink*)

MOM   No, no. Of course not. I'm talking about Marcy Smith-McMillan—that hard-working, intelligent young woman trying to make her way in the world, and you treat her so badly. I hope you know you're not going to get very far with people talking to them in that high-and-mighty way. So self-righteous and like you just know everything.

DR. MICHAELS   Go away.

MOM   I felt sorry for her, and I don't even know her. I was ashamed to be your mother—I just wanted to hide my face the way you were talking down to her.

DR. MICHAELS   I said, Go away.

MOM   All right.

DR. MICHAELS   I mean it.

MOM   I said "all right."

DR. MICHAELS   But you're not going. Damnit. I mean it.

MOM   All right. I don't want to upset you. But remember, you will always catch more flies with honey than with vinegar.

If she leaves, she doesn't go far. And he crosses to sit in the chair.

DR. MICHAELS   Okay. Dark. Dark, dark. Night. Home. A drink. A chance to sleep.

A distant phone rings and Denise, in a robe, enters to stand behind him, staring off, looking puzzled.

DENISE Hello . . . ?

DR. MICHAELS Denise. I'm sorry to call you so late. It's late, right? But do you think I overdid it?

DENISE Bob. Are you all right?

DR. MICHAELS That phone call to C.C.I—my abuse of poor Marcy Smith-McMillian—did I overdo it?

DENISE Well, honestly, I'd have to say you probably did.

DR. MICHAELS Burned our bridges, did I? Shit. I was hoping there was justice maybe, some benevolence out there in the universe listening in and it would take my side. I better just tell Frannie, "Listen, you poor disturbed, disregulated little soul, I'm sorry, but Mr. Big needs a new yacht and Marcy wants to ride in it, so you'll just have to—just have to swim the deep waters alone. It's appalling.

DENISE I don't disagree. But it takes honey to catch flies, Bob, not vinegar.

DR. MICHAELS *(incredulous)* What?

As Mom enters to watch the final moments of this exchange.

DENISE You know. That old saying.

DR. MICHAELS Ohh, for god's sake.

He rises and paces to the piano for another drink as Denise goes.

MOM Can't get along with anybody, can you.

DR. MICHAELS Shut up.

MOM Maybe it's your upcoming birthday that has you on edge. Such a memorable day. The tenth of November. Does turning forty-five strike you as a big birthday?

DR. MICHAELS (*flopping down in the chair*) Every birthday past thirty-eight feels big after all those years of thinking I'd never outlive you.

MOM (*approaching, getting close*) It was this time of year, wasn't it, that you opened the door and there I was. So sad.

DR. MICHAELS Dad once told me that you thought you were a burden to us and that you saw removing that burden as a gift.

MOM Did he?

DR. MICHAELS It helps me feel less anger toward you sometimes; but the terrible, implicit sadness in it is something I can only take in small doses. Anyway, I'm exhausted. (*sinking away*)

MOM (*watching him sink into sleep*) It was a late fall day with daylight in short supply when you were born, and another late fall day with night coming on early when you came home to find me. (*turning out, eyeing the audience*) Don't you wonder what I am, really? His mother? A ghost? Or something dark and secretive, but not her. Not a ghost. She's dead. There's a grave with a gravestone. Dates. And we don't believe in ghosts, or in demons or witches, anyway, do we. But we do believe in something else. Something far, far worse. Thoughts. We believe in thoughts. So many thoughts in our heads. In each of our heads. Thoughts racing around, over each other, under each other. Thoughts hiding thoughts. Thoughts hunting for other thoughts that are hiding from the thoughts hunting them. And all of them doing it all at once. My goodness. What a madhouse. (*prowling, searching*) We like to occupy ourselves only with the uppermost thoughts—we like to think it's from them we choose what we will say or do. Who we are. "I thought this or that. It occurred to me to tell you—or to conclude." "Our thoughts," we call them, but are they? Can we control them? Make them do what we want. For instance—stop. And which kind am I, from how deep, and am I trustworthy? Am I only a thought? Or maybe I'm a being of some kind? Of some kind of being of thought. Dark and secretive so I can get at him. Especially if he's been thinking about her. Me. Mom. (*studying Dr. Michaels*) Now is the dark hour I can stir the black pot so that it overflows, if I want, so it rises, the black, black tar, sticky and heavy over everything. It seems mean, I suppose. But if you were as dead as I am—if you were dead like me, and bitter. As bitter as I am, you would understand.

DR. MICHAELS (*asleep in the chair*)   Not now, Mom.

MOM   Poor little man. So dutiful. Trying so hard. (*moving near*)

DR. MICHAELS   Just not now.

MOM   Do you want me to sing to you?

DR. MICHAELS   What?

MOM   I could.

DR. MICHAELS   What are you talking about?

MOM   Like I used to.

DR. MICHAELS   You never did.

MOM   You were tiny.

DR. MICHAELS   I'm just in such a black, black mood.

MOM   It was before I got depressed. Before I lost hope. It doesn't matter if you don't remember. Because I do. Think back. Think way back.

DR. MICHAELS   I can't. I don't want to.

MOM   If only once when I was feeling so low and alone, and you came home from school to find me on that couch with my beer and pills, in my nightgown and robe—if only once you had sat with me and stroked my head and sung to me, I might have lived.

DR. MICHAELS (*springing to his feet*)   We did that. We saved you once. Your mind was made up.

MOM   Maybe.

DR. MICHAELS   I was trying to survive. I had to survive.

MOM   I know.

DR. MICHAELS I found you with a plastic bag over your head and a tube from my chemistry set feeding gas into you—my chemistry set, my childhood little boy chemistry set and pills all over the floor and your chest, all the pills you couldn't gobble just everywhere. I want to help Frannie Bascome. I want to save her.

MOM I hated that chemistry set. All those tubes and vials and the way you were always ignoring me for your microscopes. Like you were going to understand the world. It's funny, really, thinking of you and your little brain taking on the whole universe. Taking on all the mysteries. (*singing and retreating*) "By the light . . . of the silvery moon, I want to spoon, to my honey I'll croon love's tune, honeymoon keep a-shining in June, Your silvery beams will bring love dreams, we'll be cuddling soon, by the silvery moon."

Mom departs. Jerome inches to the piano as Barnard starts talking. Evangeline settles in her chair. Barnard carries a large envelope, as he moves to Evangeline and Dr. Michaels goes.

BARNARD So I drove straight home after last session. No shopping for me. Too risky. I felt worse and worse. Angry, you know. Pissed off. And this goddamn cold sensation that will not go away, like a belly full of ice water. So suddenly I knew what to do. I went and I bought a bottle of scotch, some really good scotch—some really pricey single malt scotch.

EVANGELINE RYDER What were you angry at, Barnard? Or maybe I should ask 'who'?

BARNARD I was defiant. Defiance. That was my flag. I used to drink a lot. So I wanted to. That's what it was, old times' sake and defiance and that's the first thing it does, the booze. It takes away the cold. So I drank, and the hangover wasn't too bad. But it made all the feelings of fear worse in the morning—it's a strange weak feeling—cold inside worse than ever.

EVANGELINE RYDER As if the inside has become the outside.

BARNARD What?

EVANGELINE RYDER   As if the inside has become the outside.

BARNARD   What?

EVANGELINE RYDER   You said that girl was attractive in a special way from the first second.

BARNARD   Attractive from the first second, yes, but more and special after the toothpaste. After we stood looking for the toothpaste.

EVANGELINE RYDER   And then you went back and it wasn't the same girl.

BARNARD (*correcting her*)   I couldn't be sure.

EVANGELINE RYDER   You were looking out of this tunnel—how did you put it—

BARNARD   This vortex, yeah, this whirlwind and I was looking out at her. And being afraid of her. Afraid of what I owe her. As if I owe her something.

EVANGELINE RYDER   Like the inside is suddenly the outside.

BARNARD   Say that again.

EVANGELINE RYDER   That your inside is suddenly the outside.

BARNARD   It's like I'm not here, the feeling. Not empty but cold and . . . (*he raises the large envelope*) I have a picture of my mom here.

EVANGELINE RYDER   You do?

BARNARD   I decided to go to the store today, and I thought it would be a good idea to look at that girl and compare her to the picture.

EVANGELINE RYDER   Do you think the girl at the market looks like your mom?

BARNARD (*removing the framed picture, he stands to hand it over*)   Maybe I can find out. It's when Mom is young. In her twenties. And her hair is dark like the girl at the store. And Abigail.

I've been thinking about Abby and that machine killing her uncle that made her stop wanting to see me, so then I forgot all about her. When we were—I thought—*Romeo and Juliet* in high school—but still real. My buddies back then lost girlfriends, and they went on to the next. Their dad would tell 'em, "Girls are like buses. There'll be another one along in twenty minutes." So they'd just take the next one. But not me. I ended up in bed until my dad said he was ashamed of me.

EVANGELINE RYDER   You're mother's eyes are very penetrating, or active. There's a sense of repose about everything else. The way she's sitting. But her eyes are engaged in something.

BARNARD   They're hard to read. I don't know what I think you can tell me. Mom looks like that girl, or she doesn't. You've never seen her.

EVANGELINE RYDER   When you watched your mom go out to the car with all those women and then go away, you said you "carried on." You cried like a baby. Which is what you were.

Still on his feet, Barnard shakes his head and laughs.

What's the joke?

BARNARD   You cannot be serious. Come on. No, no, no. No, no, no, no, no. You're not going to tie it all to that? Something sixty years ago—more than sixty that I had nothing to do with. I was just there. You have to see the joke.

EVANGELINE RYDER   But you brought the picture.

BARNARD   You talked about that book. (*moving back to sit*) I started looking at old photographs and thinking. So it's not that I'm old and my life is winding down, and it's not that I might be humiliated if I approached that girl. And it's not that I'll never get to know her, because it's all just gone, anyway—This feeling lost in time or— What is time? What the hell is it?

EVANGELINE RYDER   What feeling?

BARNARD   What?

EVANGELINE RYDER   What feeling is lost?

BARNARD   Whatever the heck we're talking about. This feeling that took me over—Abby and that machine. But you're saying that doesn't matter either. Forget it all. Because I could never find it in that girl, even if I did get to know her. Forget her, too. Because you're saying it's impossible, because it's all back in this time that's long gone. And that young woman in the photo, my mom is gone into that time that's lost, too—and that girl at that market is just some girl.

EVANGELINE RYDER   I still don't know what's funny.

BARNARD   Sure you do. You're smart, you're educated. Irony. Absurdity.

EVANGELINE RYDER   You know nothing about that girl at the market and yet you have all this turmoil.

BARNARD   I said that.

EVANGELINE RYDER   We talked about transforming every time your mom got close to you. (*crossing to hand the picture back and return to her chair*) But then she went away. So it was transforming in both directions. Giving and taking. You transformed when she arrived— with those things—warmth and presence, and then you transformed in another way when she left. So the inside she had given became the outside she was taking away. It was no longer inside of you where she had roused it—But it was outside and was walking away—in a sense being taken away, climbing into the car with all those women and driving away.

BARNARD   So it's just something about my mother—all this?

EVANGELINE RYDER   Except it isn't . . . *just* anything, and certainly not *just* mom. Or just . . . mother. It's where you began. What you needed most. At a time before language, before words, before speech, she came and she was everything. You bloomed; you were able to breath. And she went and you lost everything. And this happened day after day, and you didn't understand why, and she was gone forever each time, and you couldn't stop it. Day after day. It must have been humiliating and embarrassing. To be so dependent, so helplessly enriched, and then helplessly lost.

BARNARD   Boy oh boy. Okay, All right. I give up. Damnit. Goddamnit. I have this thought sometimes. Sometimes I don't even know I'm having it. I hate it almost. It makes me so damn sad. That when I was looking for that toothpaste and standing with that girl, and so close to her that she was blurry, it was like I was an infant who can't see well. And so it was the face of my mother—the face of her youth that I could never remember.

EVANGELINE RYDER   And yet you knew it.

BARNARD   Do you really think that's it with me? (*gazing at the photograph*)

EVANGELINE RYDER   It's worth considering.

BARNARD   Will it fix things?

EVANGELINE RYDER   Maybe such moments are visitations from time, an opportunity to know yourself as you once were and to possibly heal. But that they'll go away, too. Those feelings, those moments. So maybe cherish them.

BARNARD   This is the one for me. It pierces me. That was his word about the photo he found for his book, right? Well, this one pierces me.

Jerome at the piano begins to play a gentle delicate version of "By the Light of the Silvery Moon."

EVANGELINE RYDER (*standing*)   Yes. Well. To be continued.

BARNARD   Yes. (*they meet eyes and then she goes. Barnard turns to the audience*) And so it was continued. And do you know what happened next? I went to the market and that girl wasn't there. I went through the whole store looking for her. Just to see her and see, but I couldn't find her. When I went the next week, the same thing was true. And the one after that. And after that. I thought maybe she'd been fired or quit. But I never saw her again. She'd simply disappeared. It was like she'd never been there.

As the lights change, becoming surreal, Jerome plays on, though a surreal sound has begun as Mom enters from upstage with Franny riding piggyback, and Jerome slowly stops.

MOM Here's what I know, Frannie. When the circumstances are wrong enough, the dark push unflinching enough, it can happen to anyone. A feather, a speck of dust can push you over the edge, when everything else has been prepared secretly and against your will, without your knowledge, and beyond your rule.

She sets Frannie down, and they walk holding hands. A sense of the dangers of the world shadows Frannie's story.

FRANNIE In the book of trolls I was reading. This book of trolls, and they all have one eye. They're big and hairy both the man trolls and woman trolls and sometimes a bunch of them only have one eye between them. So they have to share it. And they do because they're trolls and they're in it together, which is kind of cool, I think. The troll who has the eye gives it away to a different troll on purpose. He gives the eye to a friend troll and then that troll can see but the first troll, the giver-troll can't.

Mom is sitting now in one of the therapy chairs as Frannie stands before her, and at Mom's instigation they play patty-cake, patty-cake.

He's blind. And there were these mean boys who tricked the trolls when they were trying to get through the forest. And the troll who had the eye got so scared that he dropped the eye and the boys took it and stole it and ran away with it.

Mom is moving away now, and Frannie is seated in the chair as patty-cake continues.

And the trolls couldn't see anything. "Oh, no," they said, "We're blind . . ."

As Mom backs away and the lights change to the reality of the center. Frannie, trancelike, is in the chair, continuing to very slowly play Paddy Cake with the air. Dr. Michaels and Nora have entered and stand on either side of the therapy chair. Evangeline and Denise hover by the reception room door.

We're blind, we're blind, we're blind.

NORA   She had to go to that hellhole for a visit even though it was after Trish knew Frannie picked me, and this is how she came back.

FRANNIE   We need to help them, Mom. They don't know where I went, or where they are, and they really need me.

DR. MICHAELS   Frannie, listen to me.

FRANNIE (*trancelike, playing patty-cake with the air.*)   Okay, Mom.

NORA   Is she talking to me? I don't even know. Frannie, honey. Come on now.

FRANNIE   Honey is from bees.

DR. MICHAELS   That's right.

FRANNIE   Big bees that sting.

NORA   They hum and buzz and fly around and make honey. It's nice.

FRANNIE   When Gregory and her are doing "all hot and bothered" they yell about honey. She does.

DR. MICHAELS   What?

FRANNIE   She yells "honey, honey," and then the bees sting her.

NORA   What are you talking about?

FRANNIE   Stuff. She yells, "I'm dying, I'm dying."

DR. MICHAELS   Do you see them?

FRANNIE   Who?

DR. MICHAELS   Do you see them? Do you hear them? Her and Gregory?

FRANNIE (*as if the idea is silly*)   No. No, no. I put myself under the bed. Or in a big drawer with stuff. I'm not even there. Just me and the trolls and no eyes. But we stick together, because that's what trolls do. And we tell each other secrets. Like about my storms nobody hears. Shhhhh. I told them and they listened. And how Gregory wanted me all hot and bothered, he's so dumb, and yelling about bees, like Trish does, but I was just yelling that he should go away, and then I couldn't even see him any more, and I couldn't see me and he couldn't either. He got so mad he couldn't see me he jumped around making a noise like a big balloon letting out air.

NORA   Goddamnit.

FRANNIE   Whatsamatter, Mom?

NORA   Frannie.

FRANNIE   What?

NORA   It's okay. It's okay.

FRANNIE   It's not okay. They took the trolls' eye, and they're lost in the trees, but I just, I just —(*stopping patty-cake, anguished, desperate*) I want some dying. I want some dying.

NORA   You don't want that, Frannie. No.

FRANNIE   I do too. There's big knives, go get one so I can give myself some dying. I want some dying and deadness, and that's all.

DR. MICHAELS   Frannie, you have to calm down.

FRANNIE   Dying and deadness are that. Nobody is more quiet. They go plop and don't even move.

DR. MICHAELS   Get Protecive Services for me, Denise. They've got to know this happened.

As Denise starts to go.

EVANGELINE RYDER   Bob, the priority is that Frannie has to be hospitalized. What are you waiting for?

NORA   I thought we couldn't do that.

EVANGELINE RYDER   This would be different. It's our move of last resort. We call 911 and—

DR. MICHAELS   And we dump her. It's called a dump. We don't have to ask C.C.I. for shit. We go through 911 because she's a threat to herself, and the E.R. has to take her. You're exhausted. Trish is dangerous. They'll move her on to the psych ward.

NORA   Okay. Sounds good. Tell me it's okay, Dr. Michaels. Tell me I can stop. It's like this. It's just like this. I tried, but I can stop. When I'm not begging her to stop I'm cleaning up the feces and urine or I'm falling asleep and waking up terrified she's gone. I jump awake. I banged my head. I don't even know on what.

FRANNIE   Where's that book? I want to help the trolls.

NORA   What trolls, Frannie, there aren't any trolls.

FRANNIE   They're in the book, and when the mean boys are coming I can warn them. "Look out for the mean boys!"

NORA   Frannie, please, you don't know what you're talking about. (*to Dr. Michaels*) What is she talking about? I never knew what tired was before. It's this whole other world. It's like—Who are you? You could be somebody. But maybe not. I know! I'll sleep! Is there somewhere I can lay down to wait? I want to go with her. I want to get dumped, too.

DR. MICHAELS   There's a couch in the conference room.

NORA   Okay. Sounds good. (*moving to pat and kiss the top of Frannie's head*) Goodbye, Sweetie. Goodbye little sweetie.

EVANGELINE RYDER   Nine one one, Bob. Now! C'mon, just make the—

Nora has moved near the door but stopped.

DR. MICHAELS (*looking for the troll book*)   She's my patient, Evangeline.

EVANGELINE RYDER   I know she's your patient, and I know why you're stalling, and I know what needs to be done.

DR. MICHAELS   Go on, Nora. You can lay down.

NORA   I don't know where the conference room is.

DR. MICHAELS   Go ask Denise. Here, Frannie. (*Handing her the book, as Nora goes*)

FRANNIE   Oh, good.

He stares at Frannie who reads.

EVANGELINE RYDER   You can't take her home, if that's what you're thinking, Bob. You can't do it.

DR. MICHAELS   I know that. Damnit. Make the call, Evangeline. Go on. Make it. I'll sit with her.

EVANGELINE RYDER   It's the right thing.

DR. MICHAELS   Can you see the future? Because I can't. If Nora bails, and Frannie's in the psych ward and they put her back in the system we might as well have locked her in that attic marching in circles two hundred years ago.

Evangeline pivots and goes, as Dr. Michaels looks at Frannie who reads intently. He sits in the opposite chair and watches her closely. Softly, he starts to sing.

"Glow little glow-worm, glimmer, glimmer. Shine little glow-worm, shimmer, shimmer. Lead us lest we too far wander. Love's sweet voice is calling yonder. Shine little—"

FRANNIE   Shhhhhhh. Can't you see I'm reading?

DR. MICHAELS   It's a song I used to sing when I was little, and—

FRANNIE   I don't like it. I can't read if you're making noise.

Evangeline enters through the reception room door, followed by Timothy who sits on a waiting room chair.

EVANGELINE RYDER Denise is still on the phone, but the EMTs will be here in about ten.

DR. MICHAELS Frannie's reading. She wants quiet.

EVANGELINE RYDER (*hushed*) Bob, I hate to ask you but could you help me out and see Timothy Archer for me? He's in the waiting room.

DR. MICHAELS Now?

EVANGELINE RYDER I know the timing is terrible, but he really wants to see you. I think it's because he knows you're a doctor, and surgeons are doctors, and the surgery on his hamster is going on right now.

DR. MICHAELS You want me to consult about his hamster?

EVANGELINE RYDER Timothy's got something stuck in his head— some kind of secret worry I can't dig out of him. And it's nerve-wracking not to know in case something goes wrong and Otto dies. I'll stay with Frannie.

DR. MICHAELS All right.

Dr. Michael crosses shaking his head to Timothy who sits holding a little photo of Otto.

How are you, Timothy? How are you doing?

TIMOTHY Ohh, you know.

DR. MICHAELS Evangeline says you're working very hard in your therapy.

TIMOTHY Very, very hard.

DR. MICHAELS And she told me about Otto. That must be scary.

TIMOTHY Evangeline says Otto doesn't know they are going to cut him, which is good. I don't think he knows. Do you think he knows?

DR. MICHAELS   He probably knows he doesn't feel well.

TIMOTHY   He doesn't run on his treadmill so much for fun now. We had fun when he would. (*holding the photo in front of Dr. Michaels*) Do you want to see his picture?

DR. MICHAELS   That's Otto?

TIMOTHY   Yes, it is.

DR. MICHAELS   He's very handsome.

TIMOTHY   Do you think so? People think he's just a hamster, you know.

DR. MICHAELS   Well, he is a hamster. That's his strength I would say.

TIMOTHY   That's right. That's right. That's his strength. He is a hamster.

DR. MICHAELS   This is very nice talking about Otto. I enjoy hearing about him. Evangeline thinks there's something you'd like to say, but it's hard. A kind of secret maybe.

TIMOTHY   No. No secrets.

DR. MICHAELS   I'm a doctor, you know.

TIMOTHY   And surgeons are doctors. They will know how to cut Otto.

DR. MICHAELS   That's right. And I was thinking that maybe, as a doctor, I could guess.

TIMOTHY   What do you mean? What is it you mean? I'd like to know what you mean.

DR. MICHAELS   I could say different things, and then if I say the thing that's hard for you to say, you can tell me. That way you would only have to say right or wrong.

TIMOTHY   You can guess if you want.

DR. MICHAELS   Do you want to give me any hints?

TIMOTHY No.

DR. MICHAELS So . . . do you want to say that you don't like Evangeline any more?

TIMOTHY (*that's preposterous*) What? I mean, wrong. WRONG.

DR. MICHAELS It would be all right, if you did. Or . . . that . . . you don't want her to be your therapist?

TIMOTHY Wrong, wrong, wrong. That's not good guessing.

DR. MICHAELS Do . . . you want . . . to . . . confess that you robbed a bank?

TIMOTHY I didn't. WRONG.

DR. MICHAELS Do you . . . sometimes . . . want to be a bird?

TIMOTHY Wrong. Wrong. Wrong. Wrong. Wrong. (*fed up, taking charge*) This dog ate my sandwich and Evangeline says the dog knows the difference, and so he knows not to eat my sandwich because it's not in his bowl, and so it was his fault to eat it. So maybe maybe maybe maybe maybe Otto knows I took him and left him with the men with knives and he thinks I'm mad at him, so he's mad at me.

DR. MICHAELS I see. I see. Well, no. I agree with Evangeline that the dog would know he shouldn't eat the sandwich that's not in his bowl, but Otto does not think you're mad at him.

TIMOTHY But what if he does?

DR. MICHAELS But he doesn't.

TIMOTHY Because I think . . . I think, Dr. Michaels, that I really love him. (*beat*) I'm talking about Otto.

DR. MICHAELS I know. Well, that's good.

TIMOTHY No, it isn't. I mean really love him with real real real love.

Denise sticks her head in.

DENISE They're here.

TIMOTHY Who? The surgeons?

DENISE No, Timothy. (*taking Timothy by the hand, she leads him out*) Evangeline will be back in a minute.

TIMOTHY Where's she going?

In the other room, Frannie hurls the book to the floor.

FRANNIE It keeps happening. Every time I read it. The boys sneak up and the troll gets so scared he drops the eye no matter how loud I shout, Look out, look out! It keeps happening, and then he can't see. I give up.

DR. MICHAELS Frannie, it's all right.

FRANNIE No, it's not. (*growing weak, curling up*) Ohhhh, god, I'm dying.

DR. MICHAELS Frannie. (*gently getting close*) Some people are going to come now.

FRANNIE Okay. Who?

DR. MICHAELS They're like nurses.

FRANNIE Why?

DR. MICHAELS They're going to take you to the storm hospital.

FRANNIE I don't want to.

She runs to Mom who has been there all along, watching.

DR. MICHAELS I'll go, too. I'll go with you.

Nora rushes in the reception room door.

NORA I was worried you'd gone without me.

FRANNIE I don't want to go.

NORA We'll all go.

FRANNIE Let's not. Let's not.

His hand on her shoulder, they take a step.

DR. MICHAELS It's so stupid of me to have forgotten this, Frannie, but . . . they're already at the hospital.

FRANNIE Who?

DR. MICHAELS The trolls.

FRANNIE They are?

As they start to move toward the door.

DR. MICHAELS They went ahead. And they're going to tell everybody about how you tried to help them and that you are coming.

FRANNIE (*stopping, pushing him away*) You're lying. You're lying.

Frannie retreats to Mom, who shoves her violently away, and Dr. Michaels scoops her into his arms and starts toward the door.

No. You're all lying. Don't make me. Oh god, I'm blind, I'm blind.

Denise holds the door open, and Dr. Michaels goes, carrying Frannie, who keeps crying, "I'm blind, I'm blind," with Nora following. Only the closing door stops Frannie's cries, leaving Evangeline alone, distraught. She turns and cross wearily to the desk where she sits, bowing her head down, exhausted. A beat. And then the reception door opens quietly, and Alex strolls in. He crosses quietly to the desk where Evangeline sits bowed over. And then he sits down beside her.

ALEX Hello, Evangeline.

EVANGELINE RYDER (*flummoxed, startled, she whirls around*) Alex. Is my calender—I'm all mixed up. I thought you were on vacation until next week.

ALEX It doesn't feel so good, does it. Being the one who's mixed up.

EVANGELINE RYDER Sorry? What?

ALEX   I didn't go on vacation. It's important to know the truth about people, don't you think? So I decided to test you.

EVANGELINE RYDER   I don't understand. You lied? (*standing*)

ALEX   It's not lying. I had a theory to test and the need for experimental data can be ruthless. It has to do with people and rape.

EVANGELINE RYDER   Alex, I need to ask you something.

ALEX   This is so sadly predictable. Of course the first thing you'll want to know is whether I'm still taking that Prozac?

EVANGELINE RYDER   I don't know what's going on here, Alex. (*as she takes a step toward the door*)

ALEX   Are you inside me?

EVANGELINE RYDER   What?

ALEX   I'm looking right at you. I'm all of me. I'm everything there is of Alex.

EVANGELINE RYDER   Yes. Of course.

ALEX   You're over there looking at me out of those eyes. While I'm over here looking out of these eyes. Don't you see how impossible that is?

EVANGELINE RYDER (*moving a little more toward the door*)   I'm really sorry, but I have another client waiting. We need to make an appointment.

ALEX   If you cared for me, you'd be free. You wouldn't care about all the others. You'd throw them out. There wouldn't be any others. (*understanding this, he seems to understand everything*)

EVANGELINE RYDER   We've accomplished a great deal together. I think you know that.

ALEX   This is worse than I thought. What are you doing all the time in that chair? Are you day dreaming, thinking about yourself for example?

EVANGELINE RYDER　I could make time to see you later this afternoon, if you—

ALEX (*calm, compassionate for the folly around him*)　No. You must see now how sad and pointless this is. Talking the way we do. What use are these things we say to each other? I really wish I knew. I was in that bar last night, the one I go to, and they were all talking. Everyone was talking all at once—talking and shouting. Drunken laughing and shouting, and it was just noise—that's all it was, and I couldn't understand a word any one of them said—and I don't think they did either. But they didn't care. And that was the saddest part. They didn't even know it was noise. And then they all went off. They went off in their cars. Back to their houses and their little rooms in the houses and their little beds in their little rooms and they lay there trying to sleep and wondering what was wrong with their lives.

　Dr. Michaels enters.

DR. MICHAELS　Is everything okay? Denise said Alex just—

ALEX (*approaching and speed-talking*)　Hello, Dr. Michaels. How are you? Nice to see you. You look terrific. Nice shoes. Nice haircut. How's the wife? The family. Is there a wife? Is there a family? Nice car. Nice dog. Nice cat. (*slowing down*) Last night this redhead on a motorcycle came wheeling up just as I was descending the stairs from that bar, and as my foot hit the pavement, his foot hit the pavement, the engine booming. I didn't want to look at him, but the way he removed the key was irresistible. The feelings he had for me shocked me. He propped the bike up and walked into the bar, begging me to follow. Desperate for me to follow. If he's a monster, or comes from a monster I don't care. He can have me.

DR. MICHAELS　Alex, I have to ask you about your medication.

EVANGELINE RYDER　He must have stopped taking it, Bob.

ALEX　Who teaches you people this crap? (*as if he must explain slowly*) You're like parrots who went to parrot school to become parrots. All right. I'll tell you. Yes, I stopped. No, I didn't. I'm taking it. I'm not taking it. I am a free wonderful human being, full of talent and sweetness and goodness and love and light. I am meant to sing whether I can or can't or the notes are right or not. Men like me. They love me. I radiate this warmth and men feel it, but men hide what they're feeling. You know that, if you know anything. And so the men who want to be with me and share my joy don't even know it about themselves, and I need to make that clear to them when I see them. The world is bright and full of light and spinning. We're spinning. Right now. I came here because—Oh, it doesn't matter why. People talk about why, as if it mattered, but we all have different whys? My why is not yours. And hers is not mine and yours is not hers and hers is not yours. It's dangerous, don't you see? You sit there in those chairs—mute—opaque—like you're not what you are—like you're more than you are, like you are not this worried, earnest—I don't know—woman, or this other one—YOU. Like you can become the world. But it's betrayal that you instigate. Betrayal of something—I don't know what, but it's big. It's of everything. I will not live as you want me to. I won't live—raw and simple under your gaze. I refuse.

Walking toward them as they stand facing him, he gestures for them to part and they do, and he goes out the door.

EVANGELINE RYDER   He was doing so well. He told me he was going on vacation, and I missed it. I—

DR. MICHAELS   It's not a simple thing we're trying to get them away from. It's an adversary of considerable cunning and—

EVANGELINE RYDER   I know. I know. Don't lecture me. You're right—it's devious. So inventive. But still. Just don't lecture me, all right. Not now. You're not my therapist. If I need to unpack, I'll talk to my therapist.

DR. MICHAELS   Fine. Sure. And you know your theory about you and your spook brought down from the attic, and that's what I'm trying to do with Frannie—I'd appreciate it if you keep your diagnosis to yourself. I mean, you can take your brilliant little theory and shove it. If I find it helpful to reference my own childhood misery to better understand Frannie I will. If I feel I want to rescue her, I will feel it.

Denise enters the reception room door.

DENISE (*puzzled*)   Hey, you guys. The veterinarian office over in Menlo just left a message that Carlotta . . . ? came through with flying colors. That's all they—

DR. MICHAELS (*his exasperation spilling over*)   What are you talking about?

EVANGELINE RYDER   Otto! Timothy's Otto. I asked the vets to let us know.

DENISE (*exiting, annoyed*)   Well, they called. He's fine, they said. Flying colors!

EVANGELINE RYDER   Not that you'd care, I guess, Bob. But I say thank goodness. The brave little thing. Good for him.

As Dr. Michaels crosses to sit, Evangeline goes following Denise and closing the door. Mom enters through the area below her station.

MOM   Oh, yes. That's right. Good for him. Good for Otto. How thrilling. You must feel ridiculous.

He sits, watching Mom, as she settles in the opposite chair, facing him.

You can be so almost—what's the term I'm looking for—help me out—delusional. Really you can.

DR. MICHAELS   You're unbelievable. Truly amazing.

MOM   Really. In what way? (*suddenly alert; then slyly*) Oh, wait, you meant something else, didn't you. Something bad about me. That I'm doing something devious.

DR. MICHAELS   That you don't give an inch. That you . . . keep at me.

MOM   I have to. All that fuss about a hamster. That's your big triumph. You work and work and that's what it comes down to. And it's not even something you did. A surgeon. A real doctor did it. And a hamster. It must be so humiliating. And Frannie, little Frannie is in the loony bin. That's your success.

DR. MICHAELS Mom. You weren't a burden to me. To Dad and me. You weren't.

MOM Of course I was. You know I was. And I still am.

Silence. They sit in a kind of face-off.

MOM (*looking off*) See that door over there?

He looks to where she indicates.

That door there—do you see it? (*Now her focus moves, as if the door were moving*) There. Right here. And there.

DR. MICHAELS I don't see any door.

MOM (*standing*) It's behind me now. It's the one I went through. And you can follow along any time you want. You can step through. It's what I did.

DR. MICHAELS I know what you did.

MOM On one side is life with its joy, delight, heartache, and steady diminishment. Make a gain—get something—have it, embrace it, cherish it, and the one thing you can be sure of is it will be taken away in time. When you get depressed, or tired—when it feels hopeless—the work, the grief, the parade of sorrow. Remember there's this door.

Walking backwards towards the area below her station, and through which she has made many of her entrances and exits. He stands at her words, listening, moving a step toward her.

Or maybe I am the door. I always loved you, and I still do. You came into the world through me and you can leave it through me, too, if you want. I'll be waiting with love.

She goes, and Dr. Michaels takes another step and stands looking off the way she's exited. Silence. And then a doorbell. Ding dong. He turns and goes to the door. When he opens it, Evangeline steps in.

EVANGELINE RYDER Hi. It's me. I saw your light was on, and I said, "Bob's light is on. Let's say hi!"

DR. MICHAELS   Hey. Look at you.

EVANGELINE RYDER   Am I a sight? Can I come in?

DR. MICHAELS   I think you better.

She carries a big purse and is dressed casually, as she'd left home on impulse without a plan.

EVANGELINE RYDER   Kindness in the night. You know. Wayfarers in the trees. What if nobody lets us in? (*pulling a bottle of bourbon from her purse*) I'm drunk, okay. (*pivotng away*) I'm madly in love.

DR. MICHAELS   What?

EVANGELINE RYDER (*puzzled, even daunted*)   Madly in love.

DR. MICHAELS   Really.

EVANGELINE RYDER   Yes. But I don't know if I dare admit who. But—(*as her gesture brings the bottle into her eyeline, reminding her*) Do you have any ice? And glasses. Or should we chug from the bottle, like the homeless do. You know. The poor people of the world. Of which we are two. (*crossing to the piano as if it were a couch*)

DR. MICHAELS   What happened? (*sitting*)

EVANGELINE RYDER   As someone once said to me—"I'm the wrong one to ask about that." But . . . okay, I'll tell you. It's the people we work with, Bob. I'm in love with the people we work with. I'm in awe of them. The people who try. The people who sit in the goddamn chair. The courage. The whole thing. Pain—it can be a gift sometimes. A wake up call. "Wake up!" it says. "You're not who you could be! But if you—if you—" We all have pain bodies, you know. And when the pain bodies talk to each other, there's just pain and frustration, and so—That's a Tibetan idea. Pain bodies. What do you think about Tibet and all that?

DR. MICHAELS   I don't know much about it.

EVANGELINE RYDER   Me neither. They follow us around, these pain bodies. Dark angels, I guess. I'm going to look into it. (*sitting* *now*) Anyway, I'm really sleepy all of a sudden. Do you have any pretzels?

DR. MICHAELS   I don't think so. But I could look.

EVANGELINE RYDER   Or popcorn? Am I being pushy?

DR. MICHAELS   No.

EVANGELINE RYDER   Just walking in and . . . you know, being pushy.

DR. MICHAELS   Actually, you're not.

EVANGELINE RYDER   Okay. (*suddenly looking around*) I left my car outside. Right?

DR. MICHAELS   As opposed to where? (*looking as if out a window*) Yep. There it is.

EVANGELINE RYDER (*As if witnessing to a mystery*)   I don't think I ever heard you say that before.

DR. MICHAELS   What's that?

EVANGELINE RYDER (*As the mystery deepens*)   Yep. You said, yep.

DR. MICHAELS   Yep, I did.

EVANGELINE RYDER   Yep. I like that. Yep. Yep. Did people say that when you were growing up? When you were a kid? Kids, huh. Being a kid. The starting point. There you are—a kid. Get ready, get set, go. (*Rising, starting toward the door*) I should go. Thanks for letting me in. (*as she staggers, but keeps going*) I'm really glad I came to the right house.

DR. MICHAELS   Actually, I see you in my guest room, Ms. Ryder.

EVANGELINE RYDER   That would be nice. (*flopping in a chair*) What's the decor? (*she mimes dialing a cell phone*)

DR. MICHAELS   Friends don't let friends drive drunk. (*watching her*) What are you doing?

EVANGELINE RYDER   I'm calling Timothy.

DR. MICHAELS Timothy?

Timothy enters.

TIMOTHY Hello.

EVANGELINE RYDER Timothy, it's Evangeline. I have Dr. Michaels.

As she hands Dr. Michaels the pantomimed cell phone.

TIMOTHY What?

DR. MICHAELS Hello.

TIMOTHY Hello. This is Timothy. I am Timothy and you're Dr. Michaels. Good news for Timothy. Timothy is okay, and Otto is okay.

DR. MICHAELS You must be thrilled.

TIMOTHY You must be thrilled. I told you so now you can know, too. I'm happy, happy, happy.

DR. MICHAELS It's wonderful news.

TIMOTHY Okay. It's night.

DR. MICHAELS What?

TIMOTHY It's dark and night. I don't want to be mean. Sometimes people are sleeping.

DR. MICHAELS Don't worry. Is he home yet?

TIMOTHY Otto is with the hospital people until the sun's up. Fortune favors the brave!

DR. MICHAELS What?

TIMOTHY Fortune favors the brave! That's Otto's motto. He has a motto and that's it. I read it to him from my book. Okay! Time to get some shut-eye, Dr. Michaels! FORTUNE FAVORS THE BRAVE!

Timothy pivots and exits.

DR. MICHAELS Okay, Timothy. Time—(*realizing Timothy is gone*) He hung up. He shouted, "Fortune favors the brave!" and hung up.

EVANGELINE RYDER He has a book of proverbs.

DR. MICHAELS (*a sudden idea makes him glance at his watch*) Do you know what, Evangeline Ryder? If we stay up past midnight—Is tomorrow the ninth or tenth?

EVANGELINE RYDER The ninth.

DR. MICHAELS Well, if we stay up past midnight and then stay up all day and past midnight again, it'll be my birthday.

EVANGELINE RYDER Wow. Will it really?

DR. MICHAELS Yep.

EVANGELINE RYDER Well, Bob, fortune favors the brave.

DR. MICHAELS Let's hope so.

Jerome, at the piano, plays an introduction to "On Moonlight Bay." Everyone begins singing as all but Dr. Michaels gather at the piano.

ALL BUT DR. MICHAELS "We were sailing along, on moonlight bay. On moonlight bay. We could hear the people singing. They seemed to say. You have stolen my heart, now don't go 'way."

Dr. Michaels scans the various stations now empty, ending with his eyes on Mom who sits looking down as always. He turns and moves into the midst of those gathered at the piano, singing the last few bars with them.

EVERYONE "As we sing this old sweet song on moonlight bay. As we sing this old sweet song on moonlight bay."

BLACKOUT

END OF PLAY